Kevin

Thank you for your amazing support throughout the years. Your life demonstrates what it truly means to show up. Continue to live full out and be a blessing to others. God Bless

Louis Moore III

SHOW UP FOR YOUR LIFE

PRAISE FOR
SHOW UP FOR YOUR LIFE

" *Andy Henriquez is a man on a mission ... a mission to transform people all over the world... and this book is helping him to make that happen in a tremendous way. This book is filled with tips, ideas and strategies to help you do more, be more, and achieve more. This young man is on fire, and you will be on fire as well when you finish reading this book!*

—**Dr. Willie Jolley,** bestselling author of *A Setback Is a Setup for a Comeback* and host of the #1 Rated Motivational Radio Show in America on Sirius XM

" *Andy is a genius and a master communicator. This book gives you inspiration and practical strategies for living an extraordinary life on your terms. This book is a wake up call to show up in every aspect of your life. If you're ready to live a more fulfilling life and go to the next level, then you have to read this book. I highly recommend it. It's food for the soul.*

—**Marlene Gordon,** Vice President, General Counsel, Bacardi North America Corporation

" *What a powerful book! Andy has a gift for crafting compelling, soul-stirring stories that make you want to take immediate action on your goals and dreams. If you have ever had a desire to achieve more in life, this book is for you. Andy provides the perfect blend of inspiring stories along with every day strategies to empower anyone to show up for their life. Read this book, it might be the best thing you do this year.*

—Errict Rhett, former National Football League player, University of Florida Athletic Hall of Fame inductee

" *If you're ready to leave behind mediocrity and start living an amazing life, this book is for you. This book resonates with me on so many levels, as I had to apply many of these principles in order to defy the odds and launch my modeling and acting career. I wish I were able to read this book years ago. You have to read this book. You'll be glad you did.*

—Garcelle Beauvais, Haitian-American actress and former fashion model, author, *I AM* book series

“ *Andy Henriquez is on a mission to change lives and that is exactly what he has done in this book. If you are looking for a roadmap to create lasting change in your life, look no further, this is the book for you. The stories and principles shared in this book will empower and inspire you to show up for your life in ways that you never have before. This book is a true guide to success and it should be in the library of anyone who is committed to living an extraordinary life.*

—**Mary Wong,** President, Office Depot Foundation

“ *This book is a game changer. No more excuses for living an ordinary life. The principles in this book provide you with a blueprint to elevate your mind and live a life of purpose. If you're seeking motivation and strategies for true change, this is the book for you. Read it and then reread it. Your life will be transformed.*

—**Dr. Traci Lynn,** Founder and CEO, Traci Lynn Fashion Jewelry

" *This is a major league book. If you're ready to start showing up and take your life from the minor to the major leagues, then you have to read this book. This book is packed with powerful stories and principles to both inspire and equip you to live an extraordinary life. I highly recommend this book!*

—Cliff Floyd, former Major League Baseball player, co-host Fox Sports Florida and Sirius XM Radio

" *What I love about Andy and his incredible new book, Show Up For Your Life is that it's real. It's from the heart. It's practical. Andy is a master storyteller, but more than that, he is a student of life. In the pages of this book, Andy is going to inspire you to show up for your life and instruct you exactly how to do it. What a fantastic literary work. I am honored to call Andy not only a wonderful colleague but a tremendously dear friend. You will too, after you finish Show Up For Your Life. Enjoy... and then pass the knowledge on!*

—Delatorro L. McNeal, II, Peak Performance Expert & Renowned Keynote Speaker, bestselling author of *Caught Between a Dream and a Job*

SHOW UP FOR YOUR
LIFE

7 PRINCIPLES TO LIVING AN EXTRAORDINARY LIFE

ANDY HENRIQUEZ

CROSSBEAM
- BOOKS -

Cover Design: Mala Baranove

Published in the United States by Crossbeam Books, LLC, Florida

www.crossbeambooks.com

Unless otherwise noted, all Scripture quotations are taken from the King James Version of the Bible.

ISBN: 978-0-9972595-3-7 (paperback)

Library of Congress Control Number: 2016901580

This book is dedicated to my mother, Marie, for her immeasurable love and for inspiring the life-changing message of this book.

TABLE
OF CONTENTS

FOREWORD

Most dreams, major projects, and history-making events never happen because the person responsible, in many cases, didn't show up. Fear, lack of courage, and self-doubt have sabotaged many great ideas from coming to pass. Studies indicate that 87 percent of people don't show up and commit themselves to carry out their ideas and work on projects because they overestimate the power of the odds and adverse circumstances and underestimate the power they have within themselves to be victorious.

For fourteen years I lived a small life. I stopped myself from acting on my dream of becoming a professional speaker. I had excuses for not showing up. I didn't have a college education, I'd never worked for a corporation, and I was labeled educable mentally retarded.

Andy Henriquez, a powerful speaker, dynamic leader, and creative author has written a book that is designed to empower you to live your life from a place of greatness as opposed to focusing on your shortcomings. He taps into the inspiring, motivating example of his mother, a Haitian immigrant whose unstoppable spirit allowed her to snatch victory from the jaws of defeat. She refused to give up even when her business was being threatened with foreclosure.

Andy, driven by his desire to control his destiny and live a life that all of us can admire, chose to step away from corporate America, become an entrepreneur, and live a larger life. Andy looked at himself while working on his job. He was well-paid and had a good title, but he wasn't fulfilled. He said to himself, "There has got to be more than this." Each chapter is laced with examples, strategies, and stories that will expand your vision of what's possible.

You have something special! You have greatness within you! This book has inspired me to raise the bar on myself, to push, stretch, and reach higher. What's your dream? If your dreams are big enough, the odds don't matter. This book will challenge you to show up for your dreams and remind you that Goliath lost! Andy will remind you that you have greatness within you, and you can continue to show up in every area of your life.

—Les Brown,
world-renowned motivational speaker
and bestselling author of *Live Your Dreams*

ONE

SHOWING UP

 Show up for your life, because if you don't, no one else will.

Andy Henriquez

MARIE'S STORY

Of all the amazing success stories that I have witnessed throughout the years, no story better demonstrates the principle of showing up than that of Marie, who came to the United States from Haiti, the poorest country in the Western Hemisphere.

When Marie came to the United States, she had less than $150 to her name. Like most immigrants, she was looking for a better life. She wanted to make her way in America and was willing to do anything she could to provide for her family.

One of her first jobs was working in a purse factory. As the purses came down the conveyor belt, she would reverse them and prepare them to go into stitching at the next station. She stood in the assembly line and reversed purses, day in and day out, without complaining.

After working at the purse factory, Marie got a job working in a hotel in Miami, Florida. She made up beds, cleaned rooms, did various other chores, and was always willing to do any job they asked of her. These were not fulfilling tasks by any means, but they were necessary if she was going to provide for her family.

Then one day, Marie got a call from her sister who said, "Hey, you know, I decided to go for my cosmetology license. I'm doing hair, and this is really working for me. Maybe you might want to consider doing it." Marie liked the idea. She immediately set about getting her cosmetology license. Soon after, she began working in a beauty salon. A few years later, the owner of the salon decided to retire. Marie bought the salon for a reasonable amount, which she had saved up.

Now Marie was officially a small business owner with a few employees. This woman, who came to the United States with little more than the clothes she wore, began her venture as an entrepreneur. She fell in love with the idea of being in control of her own destiny. Although she didn't understand every aspect of running a business, she was willing to work hard, and she made it a point to show up every day and give it her best.

The salon was a significant first step, but it certainly didn't fulfill all her dreams. That chance wouldn't come for another twenty years. Yes, after twenty years of being in the United States, she had finally found that golden opportunity. Somebody told her about a commercial restaurant building for rent in Delray Beach, Florida. The surrounding neighborhood had a significant Haitian population, which meant that it was a perfect location to open a Haitian restaurant. Marie decided to take a chance. She used most of her savings to come up with the first and last month's rent and the security deposit. She used the rest of her savings to get the restaurant ready for operation.

When Marie opened up the Haitian restaurant, she struggled at first, just as most new businesses do. She had to figure out how to spread the word within the community, keep the food quality consistent while cooking in a large volume, and provide the best pricing for the various dishes. As time passed, she started to figure things out. After two years, the restaurant became profitable. Anyone in business knows this is a great milestone for a small business owner, as many of them fail within the first two years without ever seeing a profit. Things were beginning to look promising. She had consistent customers from the surrounding neighborhood. She was turning a consistent profit month after month. Marie wasn't someone who took things for granted, but she was pretty pleased with how good things were looking.

One day while at home, she heard a knock on the door. She looked through the peephole and saw a man standing there with paperwork in his hands. When she opened the door, the man served her with legal documents. Not fully understanding what she'd received, she politely thanked him, shut the door, and carried the papers over to the couch.

She sat down and began flipping through the pages, trying to make sense of it all. As she reviewed the paperwork, she realized that it was full of legal terms she didn't understand. However, after reading over them the best she could, she finally realized that the restaurant property was going into foreclosure.

At that point, Marie was totally confused. It just didn't make sense to her because she had been paying her landlord his rent on time each month. Now she was being notified that the property was going into foreclosure and would be sold at a foreclosure sale. It still didn't add up.

On the bottom of the paperwork, Marie noticed a telephone number. She dialed the number, and a woman answered her call. In her strong Haitian accent, Marie said, "Allo, this is Marie. I have a restaurant in Delray Beach that I'm renting. I've been paying the landlord every month. Every month I pay him on time. And now I have a paper that says the property is in foreclosure. I don't understand."

The woman on the line did her best to politely explain the situation. She said, "Oh sorry, ma'am. The landlord who has been leasing you the restaurant has a mortgage attached to the property. Unfortunately, he hasn't been paying his mortgage and has fallen behind, and because of that, the bank has the right to foreclose the property."

That still didn't make sense to Marie because she was focused on the fact that she had been paying the landlord his rent every month. She replied, "Maybe you don't understand. I've been paying the landlord every month. Every month, I pay him on time."

The woman explained, "Ma'am, I'm so sorry. I'm so sorry. Although you've been paying the landlord, the landlord has not been paying his mortgage. And because of that, the property is going to the foreclosure sale."

Marie finally grasped the reality of what the woman was saying and in desperation said, "Do you think that maybe I can go to the sale, and I can ask whomever buys the property if they would let me stay? I will pay them rent every month. I've been paying my rent every month."

"Ma'am, it's going to be an investor. They are most likely buying the property because there is something that they intend to do with it, and they probably won't want to keep your business in there. I'm sorry, ma'am, but it's probably not worth it for you to show up."

Marie hung up the phone, devastated. The restaurant represented her success in America, and it was her livelihood. Now suddenly, it appeared she would lose it all. Many of us have had similar experiences—out of nowhere you get laid off from your job, you receive a bad diagnosis from the doctor, you get your heart broken into a thousand pieces, or you suddenly lose a loved one. That's where Marie was, and she started thinking to herself, What am I going to do? I have to take care of my two boys. I have to give them food and clothing and keep a roof over their heads. I put all my savings into this business. I still have to pay my mortgage and my bills. What am I going to do? And at that moment, the weight of the world was on her shoulders.

But Marie had worked too hard and had two sons who needed her. She wasn't going to simply surrender. Marie decided that, at the very least, she would show up to the foreclosure sale and see if she could convince whatever big-time real estate investor won the bid to let her continue to rent the property.

Two weeks later, she drove to West Palm Beach for the auction with her paperwork in hand. Unfortunately, the paperwork only indicated the date and time of the sale at the Palm Beach County Courthouse without specifying a room number or location. Marie got to the courthouse an hour early to give herself plenty of time to find the right room. She walked up to the front desk, handed her paperwork to the woman, and said, "Excuse me, I am here for the foreclose sale. Can you please tell me where it is?"

The woman looked at her paper and replied, "It's here someplace, but I just don't know exactly where. Try asking that woman." She pointed across the room.

Marie walked over to the other woman, but she too didn't know where the sale was taking place. She walked around the entire courthouse, going from person to person, and no one could tell her the exact location of the foreclosure auction. She spent fifty minutes trying to get an answer. She grew exceedingly frustrated, knowing that she was at the right courthouse, but no one could give her the information.

Her one-hour leeway had turned into only ten minutes. She was so frustrated, and she walked outside of the courthouse on the verge of crying. She noticed a gentleman leaning against a wall smoking a cigarette. Desperate, she approached him and said, "Excuse me."

He looked over at her and nodded as he inhaled on his cigarette. She continued, "I've been looking for the past fifty minutes. I have this property I'm renting, and it is going to foreclosure. I've asked everyone inside, but nobody knows where the sale is going to take place." Just saying the words aloud and knowing her time was running out made the tears start to fall.

The gentleman said, "Ma'am, calm down. Ma'am, listen. I am the auctioneer for that foreclosure sale. I am so sorry, we omitted the room number because we don't know the actual room until a day or two before the sale. It was supposed to be posted, but no one got around to it. Let me finish my cigarette, and you can follow me to the sale."

The auctioneer's words settled Marie's heart and gave her an amazing feeling of relief. She composed herself while he finished his cigarette. Then she followed him back into the courthouse and into the room where the sale was to take place.

Marie walked into the room behind the auctioneer, who walked to the front of the room and announced, "Ladies and gentlemen, we're about to start the bidding for the 540 West Atlantic property. If you're here to bid on the property, please raise your hand."

The scene in the courtroom looked nothing like Marie had pictured. She was expecting it to be in a room full of big shot real estate investors. To her surprise, there was only one person there to bid on the property—a representative from the bank. The bank officer raised her hand to notify the auctioneer that she was bidding on the property on behalf of the bank. Marie, who was still very much unsure of what was going to take place, decided to take an enormous step of faith. She suddenly raised her hand to be acknowledged as the second bidder on the property. To this day, Marie has no idea what came over her in that moment to give her the courage to raise her hand.

The auctioneer said, "Very well, we're about to start the bid on the 540 West Atlantic property. We'll start at thirty thousand."

The bank representative raised her hand and said, "Thirty thousand."

The fast-talking auctioneer, and the bank representative bidding on the property, instantly got Marie caught up in the action. She was so excited and, not knowing how the process worked, she called out "Thirty-five thousand," increasing the bid by five thousand dollars.

"Thirty-six thousand," the bank representative countered.

Marie realized that she increased her bid too high the first time, and she quickly caught on. This time, she raised her bid by one thousand dollars. "Thirty-seven thousand," she called out.

This thousand-dollar by thousand-dollar bidding war kept going on, taking them into the forty-thousand-dollar range, the fifties, the sixties, and eventually into the seventies. The bank rep called out, "Seventy thousand."

Marie said, "Seventy-one thousand."

Before she realized it, she was at seventy-four thousand dollars.

The bank representative upped her bid to seventy-five thousand.

Marie said, "Seventy-five thousand, five hundred."

The bank representative upped her bid again, "Seventy-six thousand."

By this point, Marie couldn't believe that it had gone so far, and she had no idea how she ended up being a bidder on the property. Even more, she had no idea how she would come up with the money if she actually won this crazy bidding war. Nevertheless, she kept going.

Marie yelled out, "Seventy-six thousand, five hundred."

And then, surprisingly, there was silence.

The auctioneer stiffened up and looked at the bank representative and Marie. The bank representative had a clipboard in her hand, and she looked at some figure on her paperwork. This time, she made no further signal to the auctioneer. The auctioneer shouted out, "Seventy-six thousand, five hundred going once." There was no answer from the bank representative. "Seventy-six thousand, five hundred going twice." There was still no answer. Finally, he declared, "Seventy-six thousand, five hundred— sold!" And he pointed at Marie. She was thrilled, filled with the adrenaline from the bidding war. Then, as the elation rapidly left her, she realized that she would actually have to come up with the full amount within thirty days.

Marie's excitement and fear overwhelmed her. She couldn't believe that she showed up to ask the buyer if she could continue to rent the property—only to leave the courthouse as the winner of the bid.

On the hour-long drive home, she experienced every emotion imaginable. She was in disbelief. She was amazed. She was grateful for this miracle. And at the same time, she was fearful, realizing that she needed one more miracle from God if she was to come up with the money within thirty days.

As soon as Marie got home, she rushed to the phone with her little phone book and began a calling campaign. She called every family member, friend, and acquaintance she could think of to tell them her unbelievable story and to ask them if there was any way that they could lend her money toward the purchase. One by one, friends and family members listened to her story. Some laughed, some cried, and others were in complete disbelief. Regardless of their initial response, slowly but surely they began to lend her money. But when she came to the end of the phone book, she was still far from reaching her goal of seventy-six thousand five hundred dollars. With only ten days left, she had only a little more than half.

Being thirty thousand dollars short was huge. By that point, she had exhausted all of her resources and options and had no idea how she was going to come up with the final thirty thousand. She prayed continuously in hopes God would answer her prayers.

After a few days with no sign of additional funds, the phone rang. It was her longtime friend, Yvose, on the other end of the line. Yvose had already spoken to Marie several times over the past couple of weeks but hadn't made a commitment to lend her any money. "I know that you have been trying like crazy to come up with the money," Yvose said. "Are you still short?"

Marie took a deep breath, sighed, and said, "Yes, thirty thousand dollars."

Yvose replied, "I spoke to my husband, and over the past several years we were able to save up some money. We know how much this means to you, and we know you have done everything that you can. So we have decided to lend you some money."

Yvose's offer was a new sign of hope for Marie.

Marie said, "Oh my God, thank you so much. How much will you be able to lend me?"

Yvose paused briefly before replying and said, "Thirty thousand dollars."

Marie couldn't speak. Once again, God was orchestrating a miracle on her behalf. Choked up and consumed with emotion, Marie mustered her strength and whispered, "Thank you, thank you so much. I promise that I will pay you back."

By the day of the deadline, all funds that Marie had borrowed from friends and family had cleared the bank. She drove to the bank and got several cashier's checks. Then she took an emotional drive to the courthouse, replaying the amazing experience in her head. At the courthouse, she turned in her cashier's checks to the clerk and walked back out as the owner of the building, no longer merely the tenant.

This amazing turn of events was only possible because Marie, who came from the poorest country in the Western Hemisphere, who barely spoke proper English, and who had no intention of bidding on the property, was willing to show up. She was willing to exercise her faith. To this day, Marie remains amazed at how everything unfolded in her favor. I know this for a fact because Marie Henriquez is my mom. She knows that her life would have been different had she not showed up.

A valuable lesson is to be learned here. When you want to live an extraordinary life, regardless of fear or doubt, you have to be willing to show up. But it's important to know that even after you decide to show up, you will almost certainly encounter challenges and obstacles. You may not get the full support of those around you. Some may even attempt to talk you out of it. And you may not have all the pieces to the puzzle.

But you still need to show up.

You have to identify some compelling reasons to show up—even in those moments when the odds appear to be stacked against you. My mom had no idea what was going to take place when she pulled up to the courthouse, but she at least knew that it was worth showing up. She knew that she loved and needed to provide for my brother and me. She knew that her American dream of being a financially independent entrepreneur was about to slip through her hands. She knew that she had something worth the fight.

And, most importantly, she knew to show up.

As you look at your life, think about the times you showed up and things worked out in your favor.

You made the right connection, you got the job, you landed the deal, you met that special someone, or something favorable happened—all because you showed up.

> *When you get into a tight place and everything goes against you, till it seems as though you could not hang on a minute longer, never give up then, for that is just the place and time that the tide will turn.*
>
> Harriet Beecher Stowe

Now, consider the times in which you didn't show up. Perhaps you were held back by fear or doubt. Or possibly someone talked you out of it. Maybe you talked yourself out of it. What opportunities did you miss out on? What are the possibilities that you forfeited? As evidenced in my mom's story, we have no idea what can happen if we aren't at least willing to show up.

If we actually decided to show up in spite of our past disappointments, in spite of our emotions, in spite of the current circumstance, and in spite of the naysayers, we wouldn't need to imagine what could have been. We would be the living proof of what becomes of our boldness to show up.

> *You can pretend to care, but you can't pretend to show up.*
>
> George L. Bell

SHOW UP AND SHINE

Either you do or you don't. Either you take action and put yourself in position to win, or you play it safe and resort to the nagging feeling of "what if."

What if you had acted?

What if you had taken a chance?

What if you had at least shown up?

Why put yourself through that? Why not show up?

Let's consider the bare fundamentals of showing up:

- *Decision.* As simple as it sounds, this really is the first step. When we decide to show up, it is a conscious decision. When my mom received those legal documents and discovered that the property was going to the foreclosure sale, she was advised that it wasn't even worth her time to show up. She had a decision to make. Either she was going to succumb to the opinion of that woman on the telephone, or she was going to set aside fear and show up. It starts with a decision.

- *Reason.* Next, have some compelling reasons that make it worth showing up. We need a compelling motive to get us through the discomfort of challenging moments. Establishing a set of reasons allows us to override the doubt, fear, or any other negative roadblock that may be holding us back. My mom's reason to show up was her livelihood, plus the two young boys who depended on her. She also could not let the chance to grab her American dream slip through her hands. That was all the reason she needed to push past any fear or uncertainty.

- *Action.* By itself, a decision is not enough. Identifying a compelling reason to show up won't carry you to success. You have to be willing to take action. As a matter of fact, you must be willing to take massive action. From the moment my mom was served the legal documents, she decided to act. What did she do? She called the number on the legal documents to get an understanding of what was happening. She asked questions, including whether she could attend the sale. Even after the woman on the phone said, "It's not worth you showing up," my mom didn't stop. She got in her car and went down to the courthouse on the day of the sale. After walking around frantically to locate the sale room, she took a chance by asking a stranger outside for help. Then after discovering that only she and a single bank representative were there, she took a bold step of faith and entered the bidding war. After winning the bid, she called friends, family, and acquaintances to come up with the money. She didn't just act, she took massive action. That's the kind of action required to show up for real.

PRACTICING THE PRINCIPLE

> *If you're trying to achieve, there will be roadblocks. I've had them; everybody has had them. But obstacles don't have to stop you. If you run into a wall, don't turn around and give up. Figure out how to climb it, go through it, or work around it.*
>
> Michael Jordan

Making a decision, plus having some compelling motives, plus taking massive action, equals showing up. This is a simple, yet powerful equation and one that only *you* can fully apply.

Are you willing to show up for your life? Do you have some compelling reasons that make it worth it for you to go the distance? Are you willing to take massive action in order to make things happen? Altogether, these three elements make up the *Principle for Showing Up*.

You may not know exactly where to start, so let's take the

principle and put it into practice. Take the time to answer these questions and walk through the following steps to position you to start fully showing up for your life. Ultimately, this is your responsibility—no one else can do this for you. It's time to take full ownership of your life and make things happen. You can start today.

Let's consider the following steps.

STEP ONE: DECIDE WHAT TO SHOW UP FOR STARTING TODAY!

You have to do away with the excuses and procrastination. I am willing to bet that you have had a dream, idea, or goal that you've put on the back burner, waiting for better timing, more support, more money, or more of something you thought you needed in order to even consider showing up.

Today, you are going to identify the one thing you most want to show up for, and you will commit to seeing it through. In other words, it's time to take a stand and make a decision that you are going to show up and finally make things happen. Use this as an opportunity to make this very important decision. Here are some ideas to consider showing up for:

- Continued education
- Financial well-being
- Starting a new business
- Finding a fulfilling career
- Better health
- Learning a new hobby or interest
- Building meaningful relationships
- Traveling
- Writing a book

Above all, don't let your ideas be limited by this list. The list is only to get you thinking and is not intended to limit you. There are endless things you can show up for. The key, of course, is to make a decision.

STEP TWO: FIND WHAT COMPELS YOU, SOMETHING WORTH FIGHTING FOR.

We know trials and roadblocks will hinder our path along the journey. That's why it's important that we establish some compelling reasons to stay in the fight. We all have something or someone that we value greatly. The key is to tie this thing or person to the goal we are pursuing. Then we'll have the drive to keep pushing through the difficult moments. These compelling reasons carry great emotional value and are often tied to:

- A loved one, such as a spouse, child, or parent
- Your values, such as hard work, faith, commitment, integrity, or honesty
- A driving force in your life, such as an entrepreneurial spirit, continued education, creating a legacy, or a desire to contribute to a cause greater than yourself

Think about what compels you and how it could drive you to show up every day. When you are motivated, you can overcome any setbacks or obstacles that may come your way.

STEP THREE: TAKE MASSIVE ACTION.

Determine what has held you back from showing up for your life in the past. Perhaps you've convinced yourself that it wasn't the right timing, you needed more money, you were too old or too young, you needed someone's approval, you needed a certain degree or qualification, or some other excuse. Now is the time to push all of the excuses to the side.

STEP BY STEP

Even if you don't have it all figured out, let's identify at least one action step you can take to get you moving in the right direction. After you have taken the first step, let's identify the next step and take it as well. When you continue this simple process of taking one action step at a time, before you know it, you will create momentum. Soon it will accumulate into massive action. The late J. P. Morgan, American financier, once said, "Go as far as you can see; when you get there, you'll be able to see farther." Don't concern yourself about having it all figured out. Focus on taking action.

Nothing significant happens until you take action. What action step can you start taking today? It doesn't have to be a perfect start—it just needs to be a start. The late Zig Ziglar reminds us, "You don't have to be great to start, but you have to start to be great." Stop putting off your greatness. Take action today and start showing up for your life.

There is nothing stopping you—but you.

SHOWING UP IN MOTION

One thing is certain—we are weakening our life's currency when we make excuses. When we don't act to create our own destiny, we are giving up, not showing up.

My friend Eula shared a story that has stayed with me, and I believe it has a valuable lesson for all of us. A gentleman named Mark worked very hard to establish himself as a real estate agent, but he didn't stop there. He obtained a real estate broker's license and opened up his own real estate brokerage office. He then hired other agents to help bring in more business.

The real estate market has a tendency to fluctuate, and during a more difficult season, Mark noticed that some of his real estate agents were lacking motivation. He came up with an idea. He placed signs around the office and sent out several emails announcing a very special office meeting where one of the agents could win two thousand dollars cash. Buzz about the meeting spread among the agents, and Mark was expecting a pretty good turnout. Everyone likes the thought of an extra couple thousand dollars.

The day of the meeting, he first went to the bank to withdraw two thousand dollars. When he got to the office, he noticed that the parking spaces that had been empty as of late were all taken. He'd gotten the great turnout he expected, and a majority of his agents showed up for the special office meeting.

When he walked into the meeting, Mark did his best to show his agents that he was fired up. He said, "I know that many of you have been a bit discouraged lately. You're under the impression that it's difficult to close any deals in this market. Sure, things have gotten a little tougher—but don't lose sight of the fact that there are plenty of real estate agents still making deals. Somewhere in this very market, an agent is generating leads, getting new listings, and closing deals. Why can't that agent be you?"

The agents looked at him and nodded their heads, realizing there was some truth to what he was saying. He said, "I feel as if some of you have stopped showing up. I feel as if many of you have stopped doing the things you know are required for success. So in order to get you refocused, I have decided to create a little friendly competition. I have two thousand dollars cash here." He pulled out the wad of cash from his pocket and threw it out on the table in front of them. That got everyone's attention!

"I am going to give this two thousand dollars cash to the first person who is able to secure this listing. I am going to provide everyone in this room with an excellent lead for a high-dollar listing. The first person to secure the listing from the homeowner will not only make a great commission on the deal once the house is sold but will also receive two thousand dollars cash just for securing the listing. Let's see who it is going to be."

All the agents in the room were given a piece of paper with the pertinent information for the potential listing, which included the property address, the owner's name, and the last known telephone number for the property owner. Feeling as if he had gotten through to his agents, he ended the meeting.

Then it was off to the races. Most of the agents rushed right out of the office after the meeting was adjourned. He was eager to see which of his agents would come up with the listing first. Based on the way they all darted out of the office, he thought one of them would land the listing that very day. The day went by, and no one came back with the listing. The following day, there was barely anyone in the office. He thought they must have all been out getting the listing and working on their other potential deals. To his surprise, another entire day went by, and no one called to say they got the listing.

At home that evening, Mark told his wife about the office meeting and the two-thousand-dollar bonus he offered all the agents. He shared how surprised he was that no one had claimed the prize. His wife said, "Of course, no one has come back with the listing. The homeowner is probably flustered and losing his mind with the all the knocks at his door and the countless phone calls he's probably getting from all the bloodthirsty agents you unleashed on him."

His wife gave time to let it sink in. "I know you thought it was a great idea, but I feel sorry for the homeowner. How could you give all those agents the same lead? They must have driven the homeowner absolutely crazy by now. He is probably not answering the phone or his front door anymore."

At first Mark disagreed, but the more he thought about what his wife had said, the more it dawned on him that perhaps she was right. He realized that he hadn't considered the homeowner's privacy and peace of mind at all. He went to bed that night with what he'd done on his mind. It was a rather restless night.

The following morning, he still hadn't heard from any of the agents regarding the listing. Feeling bad about the poor homeowner being harassed by his agents, Mark decided to contact the owner himself and apologize for all the aggravation the owner had received over the past two days as a result of his flawed plan.

He dialed the number and, sure enough, the homeowner picked up. He said, "Hi, my name is Mark, and I just wanted to personally call you and apologize. I know that you have been harassed by real estate agents trying to sell your house. I am so sorry for the number of people who have been knocking on your door and calling your phone. It's my fault, and I just wanted to say I am sorry."

The homeowner replied, "Thanks, but I am not quite sure what you are apologizing about. I haven't received any knocks on my door or phone calls from any real estate agents."

Mark said, "I am sorry, maybe I dialed the wrong number. I was trying to reach the homeowner at the following property address."

He read off the address to the gentleman on the phone, and the man said, "That is my address, and I am the homeowner."

In complete shock, Mark said, "You mean to tell me that no one has knocked on your door or called you about listing your home for sale?"

He said, "Nope, I have been trying to sell my home on my own for the past two months, and I am starting to think that I may very well need an agent. Can you help me?"

Mark, still in disbelief, said, "Of course, I can." He set up an appointment with the homeowner that same day and left with a listing agreement.

He was glad to have the listing but shocked that none of his agents had gone by the house or had even bothered to call the homeowner. What happened? He decided not to tell anyone in the office that he got the listing, and once again, he called an office meeting. This time he said he was going to announce who got the listing and won the two thousand dollars.

A good number of the agents showed up, though not as many as the first time. He went into the meeting room and said, "Somebody in this room got the listing, and sadly, it's none of you. I couldn't understand for the life of me why I hadn't heard back from any of you regarding this listing. After two days of waiting, I decided to call the homeowner myself, only to discover that he hadn't received one knock on his door or even one phone call from a single agent from this office. He was actually very much interested in selling his home because he was having difficulty selling it himself. I met up with him and got the listing myself. So, please, please help me to understand why he didn't hear from any of you."

Mark went around the room one by one and listened to the excuses the agents provided. Sadly, the majority of them all gave the same excuse, which was that they just assumed that another agent had beaten them to the punch. It broke his heart to know he had hired a bunch of agents who were not willing to show up.

NO EXCUSES!

Every one of us has created excuses and made poor assumptions at one time or another to justify why we didn't show up for our lives. Often the one who wins in life is not the one with the most talent, the most resources, the highest level of education, or the best luck. The one who wins is the one who is willing to show up.

TWO

DEFINE YOUR PURPOSE

> ❝ *The two most important days in your life are the day you are born and the day you find out why.*
>
> Mark Twain

It's hard to imagine that anyone would want to travel through life without knowing their purpose, isn't it? The average person can surely tell you the day they were born, but it is considerably more challenging for them to tell you why.

Think about your life for a minute. Do you understand what you are meant to do? Are you living a purposeful life and making the best of each day? Or are you stumbling aimlessly from one day to the next without any true direction?

We all have a special calling. Each of us has an intended purpose—a destiny. There is something, often many things, every one of us is equipped to do. We can never be truly happy and fulfilled unless we find that purpose and work toward making it a reality. No one can do that for us.

Only I can do it for me, and only you can do it for you.

Whether you know it or not, the meaning of your life is to find your calling and, more importantly, to answer that call. Without your willingness to identify and embrace your calling, nothing else in this book can be achieved.

During the course of my life, I have never been told, "Andy, it's time for you to go find your purpose in life." Chances are you've never heard those words either. You see, I was born to Haitian immigrants, and much of the emphasis growing up was on getting a good education and, subsequently, getting a good job. Don't get me wrong, those are great things to have and are what most parents wish for their children. But college and career are not to be confused with purpose.

Our purpose is much more personal. It defines what's inside us. It ties into the big picture of life, and it has everything to do with the unique reason each of us has been put on this earth. Whether you are aware of it or not, your life has a special meaning and purpose. But it's up to you to make it real.

In this chapter, we will find out how to take the principle of purpose from a simple idea and put it into practice. You'll get to take advantage of experiences I've had in my life that may strike a chord with you and help you to better understand the principle of purpose. You'll also receive the tools you need to build a foundation that will keep you on course as you begin to show up for your life.

SELF-AWARENESS

Like all children, I had my moments of misbehaving, though overall I was a pretty good kid. I followed my parents' instructions, and I was willing to go down the path they thought was best for me—graduating high school and going to a university. I graduated high school with honors and earned an academic scholarship to Florida State University. I decided to major in business administration because it was a diverse program that would allow for many opportunities. It felt right for me, and I didn't second-guess it.

Regardless of what major a student decides to pursue in college, a student is required to take a variety of core classes to gain depth of knowledge and a well-rounded education. For me, part of my core business requirement was to take accounting, taught by Professor Reimers. I was pleased to discover that I seemed to have a natural grasp of accounting. It made the busy workload a bit less tedious for me as a new student.

After my first accounting exam, Professor Reimers asked me to stay after class so she could speak with me. What? Why? All these questions raced through my mind. I had no idea what she would want to talk with me about. I sat in the classroom staring at the clock, not focusing on anything that was being said. Finally, class ended.

"You wanted to talk to me, Professor Reimers?"

"Yes, I reviewed your exam."

Gulp. I'd thought I had a decent performance on it, but my mind immediately went to negative territory, thinking that I'd somehow messed it up. "Okay, how did I do?" I tried not to look as anxious as I felt.

"You did very well, and that is what I want to talk to you about. Have you ever considered majoring in accounting?"

"No, not really," I said. "I'm going to major in business administration." I was relieved, but caught off-guard, that she was suggesting I become an accounting major. After all, I'd taken only one exam.

"Well, you should really consider majoring in accounting. You did very well on the first exam. Besides, most business owners fail because they don't have an understanding of accounting. If you major in accounting, you will always be able to find a good job in high demand. I really think you should consider it."

I left that day taking her words to heart. I found myself at eighteen making one of the most important decisions of my life. On the basis of that one conversation, I switched my major to accounting. I know that I'm not alone in this experience. Plenty of us have made a crucial career decision based on what someone else thought would be best for us.

Take a moment to reflect on your current or past career path. Did you let the opinions of others—teachers, parents, guidance counselors, girlfriend, or boyfriend—determine your choice of career? If so, you've likely done yourself a great disservice. Professor Reimers and my parents were well intentioned, only wanting the best for me, but I wish they had asked me more about what was happening on the inside.

Why not ask me:

- What are you passionate about?
- What do you believe your purpose is?
- What does a fulfilled life mean to you?

Would I have known all of the answers at the time? Probably not. But the questions would have spurred me to start pondering these matters and considering their meaning for my life. These are questions any adult in a position to influence young people should ask. These kind of questions get the wheels turning earlier so young people can start thinking about their purpose in a more meaningful way.

As an adult, how many times have you just pushed through in life, making major decisions on the basis of what those around you thought was best?

I want to elevate your thinking by asking you to answer just one question: What do you believe is your life's purpose? It's not an easy question, but it is one of the most important you will ever ask yourself. Answering it—really finding the right answer—takes some work and a willingness to explore what is within you.

After you discover your purpose, realize that it can be a long process to bring it to fruition. You will need to nurture it, pursue it, and hold on to it. What is really incredible is that your life will take on a whole new meaning based on the mere act of identifying your purpose. Even if you realize your purpose isn't what you first thought it was, you've still made a start. You ruled out what isn't your purpose and learned more about yourself along the way. That makes for a rewarding journey.

“ *Your purpose in life is to find your purpose and give your whole heart and soul to it.*

Buddha

Going through life with the sole intention of making a living can lead to frustration and disappointment. I can attest to that from my own experience. After graduating with a bachelor's degree in accounting, I decided to stay in school an additional year in order to get my master's degree in corporate accounting. Continuing to follow the advice of what others thought was best for my life, I connected with a study group of colleagues in my master's program, and we studied liked crazy for the Certified Public Accountant (CPA) exam. It was so much work, but it was what everyone else said would be best for me, so I remained committed. I was fortunate enough to pass all four parts of the exam during my first attempt and, naturally, I was elated about that accomplishment. To top it off, I landed a job with one of the largest professional service firms, PricewaterhouseCoopers, LLP. I was reaching my destination and things were looking good. The course that everyone had helped me chart was really paying off.

I started my new position with a great attitude and a strong work ethic, devoting all I had to it. But it didn't take too long for reality to set in, and slowly my frustration began to rise. I had done everything I was told to do. I went to college and got a good education at the urging of my parents. I became an accounting major at the suggestion of my accounting teacher, Professor Reimers. I became a licensed CPA and landed a good job with an amazing company.

But my early morning routine told a different story. I'd wake up to the sound of my alarm clock, rush from bedroom to bathroom to kitchen and back to bedroom just to get out of the house on time. I'd fight my way through traffic to reach to that "good" job. While doing all this over and over, like a hamster on a wheel, there was always something inside of me saying, "Andy, there has got to be more than this." And like many, I blocked that voice out of my mind as much as I could—until it refused to be silenced.

There's got to be more than this. This is a statement that almost everyone has spoken or thought or replayed in their mind. Yet it has not always moved them to discover what more there is. Chances are you have found yourself thinking or saying those words when you were going through some internal turmoil. They usually come when something has jostled you out of your comfort zone, perhaps making you realize that what you are currently doing is not aligned with your life's true purpose. Chances are that you were or are, like I was, living someone else's idea of what your life should be.

When we're in that place, it's stressful. We find ourselves going through a routine without any real thought or motivation. We sense a lack of fulfillment, and we keep saying to ourselves, "There's got to be more than this." That feeling—there's got to be more than this—is like the background noise to daily life.

Once I arrived at that point, I could no longer bear the frustration I was experiencing. I discovered an opportunity to change the course I was taking in life. I began to position myself to answer the more difficult questions:

- Is this really what I want to do for the rest of my life?
- Will I allow the fear of failure and uncertainty to hold me back?
- Am I going to continue to do this thing that is not in alignment with who I truly am?

I put off the inevitable for more than three years, but eventually I couldn't avoid what I knew had to be done. In December 2004, I built up enough courage to walk away from my corporate accounting career and begin my lifelong journey of defining and living my life's purpose.

I'm not saying that you have to go to the extreme of quitting your job to find your purpose. But I am saying you cannot be afraid to shake things up and take drastic measures to explore your purpose.

> **"** *The purpose of life is a life of purpose.*
> Robert Byrne

This part of the book is designed to help you nip in the bud any frustration you may be feeling, to stop it before it gets out of control. You don't have to keep trying to force your current situation to become comfortable. This can only result in the exhaustion and extreme frustration that I experienced. If you don't know what your life's purpose is right now, that's okay. Maybe you've chosen to ignore it. Maybe you are already trying to find a way to embrace it and make it a central part of your life.

This process will not be easy, but the load can be a whole lot lighter with a little guidance through following some simple steps.

LIFE PURPOSE PRINCIPLES

Discovering something as huge as your purpose can be painful. It can be difficult to fully comprehend. For me, it took reaching a breaking point of frustration—something I was not used to experiencing. I had always found that my formula of hard work and focus created the results I wanted. Yet the formula for finding purpose is considerably different and involves more than hard work and effort alone. There are no exact answers or routes to take, but there are fundamentals everyone can follow to guide their search for a purpose.

I challenge you to search fervently for your purpose in life. Don't give up on the process. I am not going to just send you off on your own to figure it out. I will provide you with the simple guidelines to help you through the process and beyond, to begin living your life's purpose.

To begin with, I'll make you some promises. Once you find your life's purpose, you won't need an alarm clock to get up. You won't say to yourself, "There has to be more to life than this."

When you find your life's purpose, you will realize exciting thoughts:

- This is it!
- I've been called to do this.
- I'm putting my God-given talents to use.
- I have never felt so alive and inspired to show up every day.
- My impact expands far beyond my own life.

I don't want to mislead you. I am not claiming that finding your purpose is easy. If it were easy, everyone would be living their life's purpose. Case closed. It's a journey that takes a lot of work, reflection, and discipline. Any journey of self-discovery has some challenges to it. After all, human beings are complex by nature—but we also make things more complicated than they have to be. That's the very reason simplicity is a part of the message I am sharing with you.

There's a general theory that applies when we seek our purpose. It will help you as you begin your transformational quest: Don't put money ahead of your search. You will find that when you are consumed with desire to identify your purpose and make an impact with it, the money naturally follows. Years ago, I learned that impact drives income.

Let me repeat that: *Impact drives income.*

Keep in mind that this book is not about making money. It's about discovering how you can show up for your life, how you can begin to live a life that's full and rewarding, in spite of circumstances, disappointments, and past failures.

Everything falls into place when you find your purpose.

THE FIVE FUNDAMENTALS TO FINDING YOUR PURPOSE

a. *Be intentional about discovering it.* Own your search. Being consciously aware that you've set out on a journey of discovery enables you to really connect with the idea of finding your purpose. Plus, being open about your quest can inspire others to follow your example.

b. *Realize that we are meant to use our gifts.* Your gifts can be used in a variety of ways. They can bring you joy in your personal life, as well as provide valuable contributions to your workplace. How you choose to use them is up to you. Keep in mind the words of Dr. Steve Maraboli, "You were put on this earth to achieve your greatest self, to live out your purpose, and to do it fearlessly."

c. *Begin to appreciate that there is something special and unique about each of us (whether we believe it or not).* Celebrate the fact that each of us is as unique as a fingerprint, with something to contribute to the world. It is through acceptance of this truth that anyone can make the changes that will bring greater joy, self-realization, and awareness.

d. *Recognize that something has been placed within us that only we can discover and fulfill.* Nobody else can do what you are meant to do, and it's up to you to discover what it is. This means you must grasp the opportunity to make your mark and realize that perhaps, just perhaps, you were born for that very purpose.

e. *Accept the responsibility for finding your purpose.* My destiny belongs to me, and your destiny belongs to you. If there has ever been a time in your life not to be stubborn or resistant to change, this is that time. Discovering your purpose requires a real change in attitude, behavior, and viewpoint. Any fear you may have is more than trumped by the reward of finding your destiny.

Acceptance of these five fundamentals will help you with the next section, which is focused on practicing the principle of defining your purpose.

PRACTICING THE PRINCIPLE

Only one question remains: Are you willing to do what it takes to determine your life's purpose? If you have already begun, fantastic. But perhaps your wheels are spinning, tiring you out instead of energizing you to keep pressing on. At the end of this chapter, you will find five simple steps to get you started.

But first, a few general guidelines are meant to help you stay true to yourself and not distract you from your purpose. Keep these things in mind:

- Avoid value judgments. When evaluating your gifts and attributes, don't think in terms of good or bad.

- Be excited about the transformational process. Finding out what makes you tick is one of life's greatest thrills.

- Stay honest with yourself so that you don't get sidetracked seeking something that is not based in your God-given gifts.

- Don't link your search to monetary or materialistic objectives.

- Finding your purpose is about achieving fulfillment, but it shouldn't be at the expense of others.

- Don't discredit ideas just because they seem impossible. Focus instead on opening new opportunities, not closing the door on challenges.

- Think outside the box. Going against what you've been taught by family or society or your profession is tricky, yet absolutely necessary.

- Don't force it. Finding your purpose is a process. If you rush it, you risk linking the quest of finding your purpose to stress and frustration—and quitting.

- Demonstrate your commitment. Believe it and claim it, and know that you will eventually discover your purpose.

With these guidelines in place, you have equipped yourself with the mental energy to practice the principles that lead to the discovery of your destiny.

Here are some steps to initiate your internal dialogue about what your purpose may be:

1. ADMISSION TIME

It can be tough to admit to others and to yourself that you want more out of life. Confessing that you have not been living your purpose can make you feel like a failure. But, it is the exact opposite. You are actually on the way to achieving true success.

It took me a few years of working in corporate America to admit to myself that I wasn't living my purpose. I tried to resist the idea because of the amount of time and money I had invested in my college education. Once I realized that acknowledging the truth didn't make me a failure, my entire perspective changed— and eventually my life.

There are a few useful tricks to help develop self-honesty. Start with one of them or try them all:

- Take a look at yourself in the mirror and say, "I am going to find my purpose." Say it out loud. Some of us may laugh at this and a few might find they are afraid that another person will overhear them, and that is okay. Claiming it leads to finding it.

- Write down *I am going to define my purpose* on a sticky note. Keep it in a prominent place as a reminder.

- In idle moments, repeat in your mind, "I am going to find my purpose," like a mantra. This will keep your goal of finding your purpose at the forefront of your mind.

2. EXPLORE YOUR INTERESTS

This step is as fun as it is revealing. It gives you the opportunity to reflect on interests from the past, even those from your childhood, that could be linked to your purpose. It also helps you reconnect with great ideas that you have brushed aside due to advice from others. You'll want to find a way to document or remember those interests. Document your interests by writing them in a small notebook or in a memo on your smartphone.

I remember after I passed the stage of denial and was willing to admit that I was not living my life's purpose, I had clearer directives. I started exploring the possibilities, and they seemed limitless. All types of interests, which had been lying dormant in me, began to surface again. I carried a notepad with me and jotted down all these wonderful ideas and interests that I hadn't even considered throughout the years because I was too busy simply going through the motions of life.

3. ACKNOWLEDGE YOUR GIFTS

Write down a list of all the things you are skilled at. Your acknowledgement is an important part of finding your purpose because your gifts and purpose are linked together.

What kind of gifts might you possess? Here's a partial list to get you started:

- Communication
- Artistic
- Physical ability
- Humor
- Listening
- Problem-solving
- Conceptualization
- Writing
- Coordinating
- Relationship building and/or networking
- Creative, outside the box thinking
- Logic

I remember going to a friend's book launch where she had asked one of her college classmates to host the event. Her friend did an awesome job as the host. She had an inviting presence. She had charisma, kept the audience engaged, and had a natural command of the room. Later, I saw the host of the book launch at another event. I had a chance to compliment her on the great job she did at the previous event and to mention how it was clearly a gift. She appeared genuinely shocked, as if she didn't realize that she possessed such a gift. Sometimes those around us will notice our gifts before we become aware and acknowledge them on our own.

You may find it challenging to acknowledge your gifts, but it is one of the few times that it's okay to ask someone to help you. Share your journey of self-discovery with someone, and ask for help in any gifts you may have.

4. ALIGN YOUR GIFTS WITH YOUR INTERESTS

In step two, you explored your interests, and in step three, you acknowledged your gifts. It's time to link them together and see how it makes you feel. That feeling is very important and, when you experience it, you'll begin recognizing a certain gut instinct that will tell you if you're on the right path or not. You don't have to be exact yet, but you do want to follow your instincts.

Some great ways to do this:

- Take a walk and think about your purpose. Walking creates positive energy and naturally clears away stress. It's a wonderful way to get over a slump, readjust your attitude, or find a new perspective.

- Write down your thoughts. Go old school and use a pen and paper. It helps to slow down our brains a bit and, as a result, more thoughtful effort is put into what we're doing. It doesn't take a lot of time either.

- Think about opportunities in your community to start dabbling in what you believe your purpose may be, based on the interests and gifts you've acknowledged that you have. Possibilities include volunteering, joining an organization, seeking a new job, and creating your own business, even if it is part-time.

5. DETERMINE YOUR FIRST PURPOSE TO PURSUE

You aren't going to determine your purpose merely by thinking about it. Action is required too. That's how you really discover if you are on track or not. The worst that can happen is that you revisit the list, which you can always keep growing. When you hit the jackpot with your purpose, you'll know it. An instant internal transformation will take place, and you will not be able to stop thinking about and wanting to act upon it.

I realized my purpose when I recognized how amazing it felt when I helped people create an extraordinary life through coaching, training, and motivating them to push past any limits they had placed on their lives.

PURPOSE IN MOTION

World-renowned motivational speaker Les Brown has had a significant impact on my life. I have been fortunate enough to have him as a personal mentor. I've even had the opportunity to share the stage with him on numerous occasions. When you have a mentor whom you look up to, you understand the magnitude of opportunities to learn from them and stand by their side. These learning opportunities are revolutionary, even life changing.

On more than one occasion, I have heard Les say that the easiest thing he has done throughout his career is to stand in front of thousands of people and share a message that will change their lives; thereby, earning millions of dollars and having opportunities to travel overseas and touch the lives of others. Isn't that crazy to imagine? Consider where you are now, and then imagine reaching that point of success. That's very powerful.

Aside from acknowledging his blessings, Les says the most difficult thing he has ever done was to convince himself that all he had accomplished in his life was even possible in the first place. Do you know Les's story? It is truly memorable, and it explains why he'd think that way.

Les and his twin brother were born on the floor of an abandoned building in Liberty City, a low-income area of Miami. At the age of six weeks, they were adopted by a cafeteria cook and domestic worker who did her best to raise Les and his brother, along with their other adopted siblings, on very limited means.

In the fifth grade, Les was labeled "educable mentally retarded," and he was held back several times in school. This made his classmates degradingly call him the dumb twin. That would be pretty challenging to overcome, wouldn't it? Needless to say, it took Les many years to get beyond the negative labels and a severely damaged self-esteem.

After graduating high school, Les was employed as a city sanitation worker, but he decided to pursue a career in radio broadcasting. With a great deal of persistence, he eventually landed a job as a disc jockey. It led to an opportunity to meet Mike Williams, a man he considers his mentor.

Mike shared some insight with me about what he saw in Les, which was considerably more than what the school system saw as he was growing up. Mike also saw more than a fast- talking radio disc jockey. When he watched and spoke with Les, he recognized someone with an extraordinary gift, someone who had the capacity to become an internationally known motivational speaker. This realization was the start of "Mike the Mentor" urging Les to develop his gift as a communicator and grab hold of a much greater vision for himself.

Les, however, sat on the sidelines of that greater vision for fourteen years. It was difficult for him to believe it was possible. Les went through what many of us do—he assessed his circumstances and all of his existing limitations, thinking *no way* could he achieve his dreams. Yet Mike didn't give up on encouraging him, trying to sprout the seed he'd planted in Les's mind. He hoped that Les would eventually realize his life had a greater purpose that only he could act upon.

Finally, the day came when Les did more than listen to the words Mike had been saying repeatedly. He decided to take a stand and stop running from his purpose. It just happened one day when he woke up. He knew he'd had enough of the life he'd been living, and it was time for him to answer the true calling on his life. Maybe it was time, or maybe he was tired of running. I am not certain which was the real impulse. But that day, he didn't hesitate to pick up his phone and call Mike Williams to say two simple words, "I'm ready."

That day, Les Brown's life fundamentally shifted because he decided to completely embrace his purpose. He began working tirelessly to develop his gifts and talents. He would eventually become a bestselling author, host his own television show, become one of the most requested motivational speakers on the planet, and receive the National Speakers Association's highest honor. In addition, he was selected as one of America's Top Five Speakers by Toastmasters International. All of this was the result of Les realizing his purpose.

Not all of us will have a Mike Williams in our corner to cheer us on, but we all have a calling and purpose to our life that will demand our attention. It's our responsibility to define our purpose and to answer the call. It's the only way to truly show up for our life.

> *Don't let someone else's opinion of you become your reality.*
>
> Les Brown

THREE

KNOW YOUR *WHY*

> ❝ *He who has a why to live can bear almost any how.*
>
> Friedrich Nietzsche

Has anyone ever asked you, "Why are you doing that?" You probably heard it many times as a child when you were asked to justify your actions—no doubt, right before you were disciplined! Having an answer to that question as an adult looms so much bigger, especially when it comes to pursuing goals and dreams. Somewhere in your personal pursuit of success you are going to encounter some difficulties and challenges. In those moments, your desires will be tested, and you need to be able to answer the question, "Why am I doing this?" That's why in those moments, it's crucial to have a compelling reason—a *why*—that inspires you to keep pushing forward during the most difficult circumstances.

One of the greatest disservices many people do to themselves is fail to identify their *why*. The instant such people are faced with opposition that requires them to fight for their goals and dreams, they abandon the game plan because they've never established the importance of it. They are like a captain abandoning ship when it may not be sinking, but merely is in need of a course correction.

If you intend to show up for your life and make it an extraordinary experience, it is critical that you know your *why*. It's difficult to keep the course and stick to the fight when you haven't clearly determined why you are doing what you're doing. This is one of the key principles you must embrace if you want to equip yourself properly for the project of seeing your goals and dreams through to the end. Grasping this principle and applying it consistently puts you on the winning side of the equation, no matter what setbacks you may face.

WHY AM I FIGHTING?

Years ago, a friend told me a story that exemplifies the importance of knowing your *why*. My friend was still in high school. Riding the bus home one day, he found himself in the middle of an altercation he hadn't started. Some guys started jawing back and forth, harassing another kid on the bus. For some reason, they had been determined to instigate a fight.

This group of troublemakers told some other kid that there was no possible way he could beat my friend in a fight. This seemed a reasonable assumption, as my friend was on the high school wrestling team. But the idea of a fight got everyone's attention.

The kid blew the guys off at first, hoping it would pass over and they would move on to torment someone else. But it didn't pass. They kept ragging the kid, insisting that he could not whip my friend. The kid didn't budge. Keep in mind that my friend wasn't participating in any of the harassment.

Wanting to see some blood, the boys intensified the insults, mocking the boy for being too scared to fight. *Ouch!* Those were some pretty stinging words for a young man to endure, regardless of whether they were true. The challenge had been officially laid down.

My friend had no interest in fighting this kid. He didn't have anything to prove to anyone. In fact, he considered the other boy a friend. But that didn't matter to the instigators. They wanted to see a fight, and they were willing to say anything to provoke the kid into action.

The bus finally made it to the stop where my friend got off. By chance, this was a busy bus stop where the kid also got off, along with some of the instigators. That meant the situation wasn't over.

No sooner had the bus pulled away than the group of guys began taunting the kid again.

"I told you he was scared of him," one of them called out relentlessly.

The kid had finally had enough. He threw his backpack to the ground, stormed over to my friend, and said, "I'm not afraid of you."

Now the tables had turned. It was my friend who felt challenged. My friend responded, "I'm not afraid of you either."

After a few more taunts and exchanges and some pushing, the situation escalated into a full-blown fight. My friend quickly secured the other kid in a headlock, thinking he had shown him and was going to get a fairly easy victory. Somehow, the kid maneuvered out of the hold and didn't hesitate to retaliate with a swift fist to the jaw.

In that moment, a flash of pain seared through my friend's jaw. Perhaps the blow also jarred some sense into him. He realized he had allowed himself to be maneuvered into a fight in which he had no interest. He considered the kid a friend. What was going on?

My friend screamed, "Time-out, time-out! Why are we fighting?"

The other kid paused, absorbing the question. At that moment, they both awakened to the knowledge they had no cause to be fighting. Reason returned, and they ended the fight before it could escalate further. They picked up their book bags and left the crowd behind.

This is the invaluable lesson my friend learned—a fight without meaning is not worth fighting. If you are going to get in a fight, you had better know what you are fighting for and establish your *why* upfront.

At some point in life, we all have to put up a fight. We may have to fight for:

- A relationship
- A better financial position
- Improved health
- Our goals and dreams
- Any number of other legitimate goals and causes

These fights often require us to dig deep into our strength of character and push past the point where we want to quit. The only way to attain true staying power is to be very clear about why we are fighting in the first place. Without establishing the *why*, we are fighting a losing battle—or worse, a meaningless one.

Are you fighting for someone you love? Are you fighting to fulfill a calling in your life? Are you fighting for a cause that is greater than yourself? Whatever it is that we choose to fight for in life, we had better know why. Otherwise, when we receive that first devastating disappointment that life delivers us, we'll find it becomes almost impossible to push through the pain.

My friend had the opportunity to scream, "Time-out," and it worked out for him. That was a rare luxury because life doesn't give time-outs. Even if you're exhausted, mentally tired from it all, demoralized by rejections and setbacks, life is still going to keep coming at you. That's when the power of knowing your *why* becomes crucial. You can use it as fuel to keep pushing forward when every part of you wants to give up. You'll be surprised to discover how a powerful and compelling *why* can renew your conviction and drive you forward even in the most challenging times.

IDENTIFY YOUR *WHY*

“ *Poverty is uncomfortable; but nine times out of ten the best thing that can happen to a young man is to be tossed overboard and compelled to sink or swim.*

James A. Garfield

One of the top reasons people fall short of their goals and dreams is because somewhere along the journey they have lost sight of, or flat out failed to clearly identify, why they are doing it. That's why we need to be very clear on *why*—because somewhere along life's journey, we are going to face difficulties, defeat, and discouragement. In those times, we need to stop and examine our *why*, if we already have developed one. If not, we really need to set everything else aside to figure it out.

If we approach the task in the right spirit, enduring setbacks that force us to define or redefine our *why* can be a powerful motivator.

Think of the single mother who is tired of struggling to make ends meet. Part of her wants to give up, but she refuses because of the amazing love she has for her kids. They compel her to keep up the fight and hope for a better tomorrow. They inspire her to keep pushing forward.

Consider the businessman, stressed and overwhelmed with everything in his professional environment. He wants nothing more than to walk away and find some refuge, but he doesn't do that. He stands firm because he takes his duty seriously to provide for his family.

We all need to identify a compelling reason that we can draw from—one that give us a firm foundation to stand on and provides energy and determination. We need something there for us when we have to keep pushing forward during the difficult and challenging times, when we would prefer to give up and chalk it up as a loss.

Whenever I talk about having a compelling *why*, I can't help but mention my good friend Errict Rhett. Errict was a running back at the University of Florida where he broke Emmitt Smith's rushing record. He went on to play for seven seasons in the NFL with the Tampa Bay Buccaneers, the Cleveland Browns, and the Baltimore Ravens. You could not meet a nicer, more down-to-earth guy.

I had known Errict for about five years when I heard something interesting on ESPN. One of the sports commentators shared a notable statistic, saying that less than one percent of college football athletes make it into the NFL. That statistic jumped out at me. I thought, this means ninety-nine percent of college football players do not make it to the NFL. Those who do make it to that level must be pretty special. After all, most college football players are considered to be premier athletes themselves.

After hearing that, I started looking at my friend Errict a little differently. After all, he is part of the one percent who actually made it into the NFL and one of few athletes blessed with longevity in that career.

One Saturday afternoon, while I was riding with him in his car, I finally decided to ask him about it. I was curious about his thoughts on the matter, so I said, "Errict, no disrespect, but I heard a crazy statistic that less than one percent of college athletes make it into the NFL. I was just wondering how you did it. There must have been guys who were stronger, faster, or even better than you out there."

Errict, a guy with one of those bigger-than-life personalities, got really excited and asked, "Do you really want to know?"

"Yeah, I want to know," I replied.

"Okay, I am going to show you." He began to share his story and physically demonstrate it as well. He made a U-turn and started driving to his old neighborhood in a subdivision called Carver Ranches in Hollywood, Florida. When we finally arrived in the neighborhood, Errict made a quick right turn on one of the roads and parked the car in front of a small one-story four-unit residential building.

He pointed and asked, "You see that building right there?"

I said, "Yeah."

"Andy, I used to live in the second unit… the one right over there." He pointed to the door. "As modest as it looks now, it's way better than when I lived there. You see, when I lived there we didn't have central AC. The building had a flat roof, and it was full of rats. There were five of us living in it, but it had only two bedrooms. My brother Mike and I shared a room and my two other brothers, Ernest and Stanley, shared a room."

His story had my full attention. I knew he had humble roots, but I had never heard this story in all the years I had known him.

As Errict continued, there was a sudden emotional shift in his voice, and he said, "We were raised by a single mother who did the best she could with the little she had. For eighteen years, I watched my mom sleep on the same green couch in the living room. She worked hard, long hours, and every night she would come home and sleep on that same green couch. The couch had become so worn out over the years that the center part of it had begun caving in, causing even greater discomfort for my mom. We would take pieces of cardboard and torn cloth and place them under the couch to add support to the part that had caved in."

In that moment, I was as affected by hearing Errict's story as he was from telling it. It was so raw. Before I realized it, I became emotionally involved, as if it were my own mother having to sleep on a caving couch.

"Andy, I remember one day seeing my mom sleeping on the couch, knowing that she was in a great deal of discomfort. I remember standing over her and watching her attempt to sleep on that broken-down green couch and being filled with emotion. I felt so helpless at the time and all I kept saying to myself as I stood over her was, 'One day, I am going to get my mom off that couch.' I wasn't sure how I was going to do that, but I knew that I was going to do whatever it took."

"So you found football?" I asked.

"Football was a big deal in our neighborhood, and a lot of the kids looked at it as a way to make it out of there. I decided to play football for that very reason."

Errict said that he wasn't sure what the motivation was for many of the other kids who decided to play football, but for him the motivation was easy. He had only one objective and that was to make it to the NFL so he could make enough money to buy his mom a house.

Errict was a young boy when he first had that thought. He faced a long journey through the football system—youth football league, high school, college, the pros—to make that happen. Along the way, there were many times when things became difficult for him. He experienced injuries, dealt with competition from stellar athletes, and, at times, thought about quitting.

The one thing that always kept him going, the one thing that motivated him to outwork everyone else on the football field, the one thing that always pushed him past the pain was the burning desire to get his mom off that couch. His desire gave him the energy and focus to stay the course on his long and difficult journey. Without that fierce ambition to get his mom off the couch, Errict might not have had the discipline or the willingness to do the hard work. But he did have it and, as a result, he made a name for himself as one of the greatest running backs to come out of the University of Florida.

In 1994, during the second round of the NFL draft, Errict was accepted by the Tampa Bay Buccaneers. When he received his signing bonus, there was no question about what he was going to do with it. His focus was not on himself. He used that money to purchase his mom a beautiful home, over 4,000 square feet with a three-car garage. After a long, tough journey, Errict got his mom off that green couch. It had taken him about fifteen years, but he had done it. He never lost sight of his *why*.

You may not have a mom sleeping on a broken-down green couch, but you still need a powerful *why*. You should have a compelling reason that will help you stick to the fight, no matter how difficult things get or what obstacles you have to overcome. All you have to do at this point is identify your *why*. Without it, you may find it impossible to see your goals through to the end.

What is the one thing that makes it worthwhile for you to keep pushing forward even during those times when you want to give up the fight? What are you willing to put it all on the line for?

IT ALL STARTS WITH A *WHY*

❝ | *Things may happen around you and things may happen to you, but the only thing that really matters is what happens in you.*

Elise Robinson

Our environments certainly are influential factors in our lives, choices, and approaches to almost everything we encounter on a day-to-day basis. What goes on inside us, however, carries far more influence. Our internal workings really drive everything we are capable of doing. Without thorough self-knowledge, we cannot hope to initiate the process of showing up—a process that truly makes the difference in our lives regardless of circumstances. It's the game changer, the one thing that puts everything else into perspective. And it all starts with a **WHY**.

<u>W</u>atching is not an option.

<u>H</u>oping alone is not enough.

<u>Y</u>ou are the difference.

You can listen to and read all the positive self-help material available and think about what you want to change until you're blue in the face. But if you do not take action, those changes are not going to happen.

WHY helps make action possible.

WATCHING IS NOT AN OPTION.

This is a fundamental principle of showing up. You can't get ahead just by watching. Someone once said, "There are three types of people in this world: those who make things happen, those who watch things happen, and those who wonder what happened." Which do you want to be? When you decide to show up, you can no longer be a spectator of your life. You can no longer sit back and watch things happen *to* you. You have to be an active participant in making your dreams become a reality.

Errict Rhett didn't get his mom off the green couch simply by watching other athletes play football. He had to get in the game, develop his skills, and outwork those around him. When we have a *why*, we understand that watching others while we sit on the sideline is not an option.

HOPING ALONE IS NOT ENOUGH

Genuine hope is a great thing, giving us the faith to keep going. But hope alone is never enough.

We hear so many people talking hope instead of action. They say, "I hope that things will change for the better," instead of putting in the effort to make things actually change for the better. If you truly want to change your life, why not do something about it? Others say, "I hope this is my year to find that special someone." Then they do nothing different to prepare themselves for that person or to put themselves in healthy environments to increase their chances of crossing paths with that person. Instead, they remain hopeful it will happen despite a lack of effort.

It would be awesome if we could get everything we wanted out of life simply by hoping for it. Instead, we have to affirm hope by taking action and doing the work. Hope for the future can give you power in your present situation, but that power should be used to take action.

Errict had hopes of getting his mom off the green couch, but he knew that hope alone would never be enough. His hopes only became reality through focus and a relentless work ethic. Hope is powerful, but we have to be willing to put in the work.

YOU ARE THE DIFFERENCE

Circumstances are always happening around you. Often, those circumstances challenge your plans, goals, or desires. Circumstances make you search for the solution—not realizing that you *are* the solution. You are the difference maker. When you clearly identify your *why* and become willing to take action, nothing can keep you from making things happen.

Don't buy into the notion that you're a victim of circumstances or that your fate lies in someone else's hands. You can do so much more than you can imagine. But if you want to fulfill all this potential, you have to identify your *why* and allow it to move you forward. When you harness the power of your *why*, you come to realize that ultimately the difference is you.

At times, it seems easier to focus on what's wrong instead of identifying what makes it worthwhile to make things right. We can get caught up in the blame game. It is the economy, the politicians, a lack of resources, the lack of support—the list can go on and on. The reality is no matter what the circumstances, we can overcome obstacles if we have a clear and compelling *why*, if we are willing to pay the price.

Because you've read this far without giving up, I believe you're willing to pay the price.

Now let's work on identifying and leveraging your *why*.

PRACTICING THE PRINCIPLE

You should be intentional about identifying what you want out of life. It's just as important to identify why you choose to pursue the things you want. By now, you have probably discovered that life has a way of slinging challenges and distractions that are sure to knock you off course when you aren't clear on what you want. You are also thrown off course if you have failed to identify what makes it worth it for you to stick it out and overcome the challenges. You are capable of great things when you have a clear vision and have identified compelling reasons to fight. Let's consider the following questions:

1. *What is your ultimate goal at this time?*

It's hard to live a fulfilling life when you haven't taken the time to identify what you want. You need a clear goal, something worth pursuing. Sometimes you set goals you lack the motivation to accomplish. Often those goals are not aligned with your purpose or the values that are most important to you.

Reflect on your life right now and think about what's most important to you. Plus, what are you looking to accomplish? Here are some common goals to consider. Please do not limit yourself to these. Is there anything on the following list that you want?

- Starting your own business
- Going on a vacation
- Saving money for your children's college education
- Learning a new skill or finding a new career
- Being able to take a week off without worrying about money
- Finding that special someone to share your life with
- Getting out of debt
- Getting in better shape or eating healthier

These are some common goals that many people have. How about you? What do you want?

2. *What goal are you most willing to commit yourself to?*

You can certainly go after multiple goals at the same time. But when you are creating a significant change in your life, it takes narrow focus and a series of baby steps that, in turn, create momentum and lead you to a breakthrough. If possible, focus on one major goal at a time, developing some progress that you can build on in other parts of your life. No more excuses and procrastinating.

Some things to consider when choosing the major goal you're committing to:

- What is the true motivation behind this goal?
- Is this something that originated from you or are you chasing someone else's dream?
- Will you commit to doing whatever it takes to see things through until the end?

It's essential to ensure that you are picking a goal worth

striving toward. Some thoughtful reflection can help you make the best choice. Remember, it won't always be easy, but it is a whole lot easier when you have the clarity and drive to make it happen.

3. *How do you plan to stay focused on your why?*

When you first set out to reach a major goal, you're excited—no, euphoric—about the possibilities of changing for the better. Invariably, daily life steps in. Distractions small and big intrude, testing your willpower and discipline. So many tiny things arise and need to be addressed right away! Your car breaks down on the way to that important meeting. One of the kids is home sick. It starts pouring rain when you decide to go out jogging. You get hit with an unexpected expense while you're attempting to save money.

Before you know what happened, that all-important, life-changing goal gets pushed to the back burner, where it simmers untended until the pot boils dry. But hey, you'll get back on track tomorrow, right?

What this approach overlooks is that tomorrow never comes. It's always about today.

When this happens, you need a way to keep things in perspective and regain focus. You need a way to remind yourself that what you are doing is important. You need an attitude adjustment—or readjustment.

For my friend Errict, it wouldn't have been realistic to haul that green couch around as a reminder of his principal goal. Instead, he kept the image of his mom sleeping on the green couch in his mind.

What can you do to keep your *why* at the forefront of your mind? Consider the following questions.

1. *What mental triggers can you give yourself when you're tired from the fight?*

You need a reminder to restore your commitment and

motivation. It can be a powerful image, a saying you love, a song, or simply the presence of those who are most important to you.

2. What actions can you take consistently to help you achieve what you want?

Determine what actions you can do monthly, weekly, and daily—whether you feel like doing them or not. Sometimes we lose sight of what is most important to us because we aren't acting on it consistently. If we're working toward a goal on a regular basis, we'll find that our drive begins to grow until we no longer have to think about it—it's just automatic! Our desire and belief system begins to intensify because our goal is something we are consistently pursuing. Don't be casual in your approach either. Remember how important this goal is to you and work at it every day.

Errict played football for a significant part of the year for over a decade, but even during the off-season, he was still training and conditioning. It was hard for him to lose sight of his goal because he constantly engaged in activities to pursue that goal.

3. What should you do when you have dropped the ball?

Remember, you're a human being. Every once in a while you are going to drop the ball, miss the mark. You're going to fail to make a consistent effort. The key is how you respond when you realize you have lost track of the goal. Will it be used as an excuse to come to a complete stop? Are you going to think, "What's the use, I'll never get what I want!" Will you take advantage of the situation? "Well, I've been slacking off for three weeks, so I'll wait until Monday, next month, or next year to buckle down again!" Will you let this type of thinking rob you of your focus or diminish the importance of what you are doing?

Believe it or not, there are times when a splash of guilt is just the motivator you need. It can serve as a reminder that it's time to redirect your focus to what is important and must be done. In those moments, rather than beating yourself up, divert your attention back to your *why*, renewing that laser-like concentration. Take immediate action to rebuild the momentum again. After all, this is something you already have established as an absolute must to accomplish. If you want to achieve the kind of life you desire, no real shortcuts exist.

4.   *What type of milestones can you create for yourself?*

The journey toward improvement can feel like there is no end in sight. Remain diligent in pursuit of your goals by setting benchmarks along the way. Acknowledge your progress now and then so you don't become discouraged. Set milestones to remind yourself that you are in fact making progress.

Goals such as getting out of debt, operating a profitable business, obtaining a degree, and so forth can take years. You don't want to get caught up in the length of time it takes to reach your goal. That can cause you to lose sight of the reason you started in the first place.

It becomes that much more important to identify and remain focused on your *why* when you have goals that require longer periods of time to accomplish. The key is creating milestones to monitor your progress and acknowledging the fact that each milestone means you are that much closer to your goal.

At one point, Errict's goal was simply to make it on the youth football team. Then his goal was to make it on the high school football team. Next came a starting position on the high school football team. After that it was to earn a college football athletic scholarship, then a starting position on the college football team, and ultimately, to perform well enough to get drafted in the NFL. When you are pursuing a long, difficult, ongoing goal like Errict's, it's important to establish benchmarks along the way so you can remain focused.

Knowing your *why* is such a revolutionary part of this process. It gives you that grit to keep going regardless of what is taking place in the world around you. It helps you take pride in each milestone, instead of focusing on how much is yet to be done. But while a solid grasp on your *why* is a driving force in your successes, the lack of *why* is an opposing force, the one that keeps you stagnant or makes you topple backward. Stand strong and remain loyal to your objectives by understanding your *why*.

WHY IN MOTION

>   **" "** | *The heart of human excellence often starts to beat when you discover a pursuit that absorbs you, frees you, challenges you, or gives you a sense of meaning, joy, or passion.*

Terry Orlick

As a child, it wasn't uncommon for me to drift out of my mom's sight when we went to a department store. You know how kids are. I would hide in the clothing rack, wander away as something caught my eye, and not really concern myself about where my mom was. But she knew how to get me back in sight, pronto. My mom would look sternly in my direction, shout my name, and say, "Come over here. You remember what happened to Adam."

Adam was a six-year-old boy who came from a city near where we lived in Florida. One day, he was at a department store with his mom, Reve, and he left her sight for just a few short minutes to check out the video games. Those short minutes turned to tragedy. He was never seen alive again.

The sad incident struck fear in the hearts of parents across America as it made national news. Abducted by a serial killer, Adam was found dead a few weeks later. Can you even begin to imagine the grief his parents must have gone through? Sadly, Adam's death could not be reversed. But it gave birth to an extraordinary and compelling *why* in his parents.

Years later, I discovered that the man who was the host of one of my mom's favorite shows *America's Most Wanted* was John Walsh, Adam's father. After his son disappeared, John discovered there was no set protocol for when a child goes missing in a department store. He realized that his son's life could have possibly been saved with faster emergency response. John Walsh had received an extraordinary *why*—to protect and save as many other children as possible. He couldn't save his own son, but he became the single greatest voice for missing and exploited children.

John and Reve Walsh worked tirelessly as advocates for child victims. Their efforts resulted in Code Adam, a national missing child program in the United States and Canada, named after their son. Under Code Adam, if a visitor in a department store reports a child missing, a description of the child is obtained, and all exterior access to the building is locked. The employees become involved in a search and many other enhanced emergency responses are implemented to increase the probability of recovering the lost child. This was an amazing achievement, but the *why* still hadn't been fully addressed for John Walsh.

John's tireless drive also led to the launch of *America's Most Wanted*, the longest-running crime reality show of its kind. The show has resulted in the capture of over one thousand of the most wanted fugitives in America. John, who had been in the hotel management business when his son was abducted, took on a whole new purpose in life. He embraced a *why* that permeated the core of his soul.

John has dedicated his life to being one of the leading voices to help missing and exploited children. I have had the honor of hearing him share his story firsthand at a conference, and there is no doubt that his success and impact is a result of having a powerful, heartfelt *why*.

No one would want to discover their *why* at the price John paid. But regardless of the circumstances, we all have the capacity to find a *why* sufficiently compelling to enable us to do something extraordinary with our lives—each and every one of us.

What's your *why*, and how will you use it to do something extraordinary with your life?

FOUR

ANTICIPATE THE HITS

> " *Beloved, think it not strange concerning the fiery trial which is to try you, as though some strange thing happened unto you.*
>
> 1 Peter 4:12

Perhaps, one of the more painful moments is when you realize you should have seen something coming. Can you always prevent bad things from happening? No. Everyone takes a punch on occasion. But some of those punches can be anticipated. A difficult event or circumstance may still knock you down, but you can recover much faster, if only you see it coming. And sometimes, if you are really lucky, maybe you can avoid the train wreck altogether. Unfortunately, we easily grow complacent, and that's when we stop anticipating the hits in life.

I am sure you have experienced one of those unanticipated hits in your life. Boom! Out of the blue, something happened and, for one reason or another, you didn't foresee it. Even worse, you just weren't mentally prepared to deal with it. It leaves you standing there in shock for a moment. Maybe you beat yourself up for a little while—or a very long while. At the very least, it disrupted your life and likely put you into a funk.

These situations can make you feel:

- Helpless
- Stupid
- Defeated
- Depressed

Do they have to make you feel that way? Absolutely not! Learning to anticipate the hits in life and taking on those unpleasant incidents head-on is a sign that you are showing up for your life. You are not playing it small anymore.

Mike Tyson comes to mind every time I talk about this topic, either one-on-one or to an audience. His boxing career and personal life may be filled with controversy, but Mike Tyson is nonetheless one of the great heavyweight boxing champions of all time. His skills and presence in the ring demanded attention from people, even those who weren't boxing fans.

As a young man, I had the opportunity to see Mike Tyson fight. I wanted to get as close to the action as possible, so I moved up near the television screen, ready to watch him unleash his fury on his opponent. Other fighters usually had no idea what hit them—Tyson knocked many of his contenders out cold in the first round. His tremendous power in the ring sealed his legacy as a boxer, but it left many fans disgruntled. They paid big bucks to watch a title fight in a swank Las Vegas arena, or some equally glitzy place, and they seldom felt they got their money's worth. The fight was over that fast.

Tyson compiled an impressive professional record of 37–0 prior to his first loss on February 11, 1990 to underdog James "Buster" Douglas. It was a shocking upset to everyone, including the crowd in Tokyo where the fight took place.

Anytime a superstar dominates a sport, competitors work hard to find weaknesses and expose them. It happens in every sport—ask Wayne Gretzky, Michael Jordan, or Barry Bonds. For Tyson, opponents entered the ring after spending countless hours with their coaches, developing strategies that might defeat the champ. There were a variety of theories, including: he lacked technique and could be out-boxed; his previous opponents had been cowards, made fearful from all the hype about his lucky knockouts; he hadn't faced an opponent with heart yet; or his endurance had never been truly tested because his fights ended so fast.

There was reason after reason why Tyson shouldn't be the best. But every opponent who climbed into the ring to test this or that reason went down like a timber in the forest. Tyson rang the bells with a flurry of punches, and then the referee ended the fight, awarding the champ another technical knockout.

> " *Everybody has a game plan until they get hit.*
>
> Mike Tyson

Can you imagine how Mike Tyson felt hearing all the reports and comments of how people were so eager to come after him and knock him off his boxing throne? Regardless of physical toughness, he needed mental willpower to maintain his focus and continue to prove people wrong. Tyson showed he was different from the other professional heavyweight boxers in the mental toughness arena. He countered is detractors with a simple, profound statement, "Everybody has a game plan until they get hit." I love that quote because its relevance extends far beyond the boxing ring. It defines what happens in real life.

ADAPTING TO THE GAME PLAN

Whether we write it down or not, at some point, we formulate a game plan for our lives. We envision the kind of life we want, the type of relationships we want to have, the type of career or business we want, the places we want to go, and the things we want to acquire. We think we have it all planned out, and we embark on our journey in pursuit of success. Then, our personal "Mike Tyson" comes along and delivers a devastating blow that stops us cold. It skews our vision, and we're left staring into space with no idea where to go or how to respond. An old boxing adage says, "It's the punch you don't see coming that knocks you out."

Don't we understand this far too well?

Some of the most shocking "I didn't see (or acknowledge) it coming" moments are:

- Being let go from a job (fired or laid off)
- A failed marriage
- Unexpected health issues
- A sudden financial setback
- A newly formed addiction
- The death of a loved one

The list could go on and on, as life has the ability to hit us in so many different ways. It is a part of our human experience and something that we cannot avoid.

The Bible, the bestselling book of all time, has a verse that contains this statement, "In this world you will have tribulation." John 16:33 (NKJV) Notice the word *will*. Not that you have a fifty-fifty chance of encountering trials or only a slight probability of tribulation. It clearly states that you will have challenges. Knowing this makes it very logical to find a way to anticipate the hits, doesn't it?

Why let those unforeseen blows take you out and lead you to abandon the game plan you desire for your life? Those hits may slow you down, and often, they will hurt, but they don't have to take you out. We have to build up our mental strength and know that life is going to hit us with some things that we didn't necessarily anticipate. When they present themselves, we have to deal with them to the best of our abilities and keep pushing forward.

> **Life is 10 percent what happens to you and 90 percent how you react to it.**
>
> Charles R. Swindoll

Once you accept the fact that you can't avoid experiencing hits in life, you are free to shift your focus to what you can control. You begin to take back your power. You can't control what happens in life, but you can control how you respond—to any situation. It's a matter of letting go of what you cannot control and focusing on what you can.

Every time something bad happens to you, you make a choice. You either work through it, or you waste energy working against it. I know from experience that one of the best ways to prepare for the blows in life is to anticipate them. This doesn't mean you walk around with a negative attitude, expecting some disaster to fall on you any minute. If you did, you'd be likely to say, "Why bother trying to get ahead? It's only going to be taken away."

Such an outlook does nothing to help you show up for your life. When you are pursuing your goals and dreams, you want to be mentally prepared for the difficulties and disappointments you will encounter. In other words, you should expect to be tested. Something is going to happen that challenges you at some point in your life and forces you to dig deep for that grit to persevere and keep moving forward.

Think about the hero wounded in battle, still doing everything he or she can do to keep moving forward. Part of their strength comes from mental preparation. They've trained for the possibility of getting wounded, and they understand that a mission remains to be accomplished. You have to be that type of hero in your own life and have the mental fortitude to complete your own personal mission. You need to show how badly you really want it.

Anticipation is everything. A mentally prepared mind, along with a relentless no-quit attitude, keeps your motor running instead of locking you up and bringing you to a screeching halt. Imagine how much more powerful your potential becomes when you:

- Rebound from unforeseen setbacks quickly
- Believe that you can overcome any challenge or obstacle
- Refuse to let the hits stop you, but instead use them for strength

- Gain confidence that you can take the right actions to counteract those hits that life delivers

People get sidelined in life when they don't anticipate the hits. The moment they are released from a job, lose money from a bad investment, receive a bad diagnosis from the doctor, suffer a broken heart, or experience any other significant hit in life, they spiral into a state of depression or fear and become paralyzed. Instead of recovering, they choose to surrender. This only delays their recovery time and puts them in a state of helplessness. We get to that place where we focus on all the things we cannot change rather than mentally equipping ourselves to work on the things we can change.

How do you handle the hits? Think about that a moment. If you're honest with yourself, you'll likely see that you've made some situations in your life tougher than they had to be instead of accepting them and seeking resolutions. In a way, you knocked yourself out.

I'm not telling you to do anything that I don't actively apply to my own life. I learned about anticipating the hits the hard way. I experienced a hit that many people have had in life, a financial hit. It was 2004, and I had just built up enough courage to resign from my accounting job in corporate America. Financial responsibility was something that had always been ingrained in me by my family. We have always believed in saving and living below our means.

During my years of working at a corporate job, I kept my expenses low, and I had saved what I thought was a significant amount of money for someone in their twenties. I was feeling confident about my finances, which is part of the reason why I had the courage to walk away from a career that was rewarding financially, although not emotionally. I was eager to prove that I could make it as an entrepreneur, especially since the majority of people thought I was crazy for leaving my profession. I wanted to prove them wrong and felt no doubt about doing so. I sought opportunity and, sure enough, within a few short weeks, it presented itself.

A family friend called me on the phone and told me that he

wanted to come by to talk about an investment opportunity. I was more than eager to hear about it. I wanted to explore every avenue of becoming a successful entrepreneur. I was open to all ideas, not wanting to cast any aside without first considering them. A pitchman couldn't have had a more receptive audience.

We scheduled a time for him to come over with his presentation. I'll never forget how it unfolded before me that day. We sat down at the breakfast table, where he opened a folder and spread out all these beautiful, vibrantly colored brochures.

He was clearly excited, and I was drawn to the beauty of what he was showing me. With great enthusiasm, he started talking to me about Costa Rica. He said, "Costa Rica is going to be the next retirement destination, Andy. It's beautiful, the people are wonderful, the cost of living is low, and because of this, the demand for housing on that beautiful island is going to be high."

I didn't say much. What he said made sense to me, and housing demands for an increasing population is a simple concept to grasp, "That means that there is a great opportunity for investors."

"How so?" I asked.

He responded with more detailed information, happy that I was asking questions and not shaking my head. After all, a great entrepreneur never says no without all the facts. He said, "This is what we can do. I have located a piece of land in Costa Rica that we can develop. We simply have to purchase the land and place manufactured log cabin homes on it. We only need to purchase three log cabins homes up front for $7,000 each, and we will present them as the models for the subdivision. When people come to see the model cabins, we will offer them for purchase for $21,000. We will require a $7,000 deposit upfront for the cabin, and the rest, minus a few other expenses, will be profit. To make it even better, we are not going to sell them the land. They will rent the land from us on a yearly basis. What do you think, Andy?" He was excited, and he looked at me to see if my eyes were lit up.

The Costa Rica plan sounded pretty stellar to me. It made perfect sense, and I began to share his excitement. As I flipped through his brochures, I saw how Costa Rica would be an easy country to fall in love with. It was breathtaking. Then I looked at his handwritten development plan, asked him a couple of questions, and he answered with solid responses. He had really researched everything and had a lot of knowledge. The next thing I knew, my excitement had taken me online, and I was booking a flight to Costa Rica to finalize the deal. I was an entrepreneur in the making.

I fell in love with Costa Rica. Everything that he said appeared to be true. I toured the area and met awesome people. I discovered firsthand that the cost of living was fairly low, and I met quite a few foreigners who frequented Costa Rica, many of whom planned to retire there.

We drove around and checked out the various lots for sale. They all looked beautiful, and I could just imagine how a log cabin home would look on them—absolutely gorgeous and an ideal way to spend retirement years. When we visited the log cabin manufacturer, I was impressed with its facilities and operations. By the time we left, eager to reach the attorney's office to draw up the agreement, I had every confidence the project was an amazing opportunity.

The trip went by entirely too quickly, and I left Costa Rica feeling content and fulfilled. I sensed that I had made a great decision, and I couldn't wait to watch it play out. I was elated on the trip back home, thinking about how I was going to be living my dream. I would be an accomplished entrepreneur; someone others would admire. If I could have patted myself on the back, I would have.

Within a few days of returning, I got a call from the family friend who reiterated that I had possibly made the best investment I could ever make with my $40,000 in savings. I already believed that, but hearing him say it made me excited all over again. All that was left to wonder about was how long it would take to make a return on my investment.

For the next two weeks, I heard from him every few days, getting updates on how everything was coming along. It was fantastic. Then about a week went by, and I didn't hear from him at all. I really didn't think much about it. After all, how many investors get weekly updates on what's happening? When you're taking care of business and earning money for your investors, you need to remain focused. Two more weeks passed. I thought this was a little strange, but again, I figured he must be busy, and I let it ride.

By week four, I decided that I should probably give him a call. I phoned him several times using a calling card, but I didn't get any answer. Over the next days, I tried a few more times, but there was still no response. I couldn't deny that something didn't feel right. He had been an excellent communicator until the past four weeks. The man I had worked with on my big opportunity had not been someone who simply didn't respond. Suddenly, I couldn't get in touch with him. It made no sense.

For the next two weeks, I was in a frenzy trying to reach this guy and having no luck. I had no idea what to do, and short of going to Costa Rica to literally track him down, my options were limited. I tried calling him all times of the day. As you can imagine, my sleep suffered and my mind was so distracted, wondering what was going wrong. One day, I finally got a breakthrough.

He answered the phone, and I was relieved. You know how it is when you can't get in touch with someone. You begin to fret that something has happened. I said, "Serge, what is going on? I haven't heard from you in a long time, and I have been calling you nonstop for the past couple of weeks."

He said, "I know, I am so sorry."

Apologies are good, but I needed information, not an apology. I said, "What do you mean you are sorry? What is going on?"

He replied, "I feel terrible, and I didn't know how to tell you that I lost your money. Another opportunity came up, and I took some of my money and your money to invest in it. I thought everything would work so we would have additional money for our development project. But everything went terribly wrong, and I lost your money."

This was not the information I had wanted to hear. "You've

got to be kidding me," I said, feeling instantly ill. "How much of my money did you lose?"

I waited for his response, and he said, "All of it."

"All of it," I repeated, hoping I had heard him wrong. The silence on the other end of the line told me I hadn't.

I couldn't muster up any more words to speak to him, so I spared myself the details and hung up the phone. Flopping into the nearest chair, I felt as if I had been hit with a bag of bricks. I began thinking about how long it had taken me to save that money. Then I tortured myself further by replaying all the events that had happened. Anxiety and remorse began to cost me sleep, peace of mind, and happiness. I was completely stressed out.

It didn't take long for me to start beating myself up. I was thinking, "I just left corporate America. What am I going to do?" My pride had taken a hit too. I was embarrassed about my naiveté when it came to the opportunity and how I pursued it. I thought I had been careful, but what did I miss?

Then I started to think I had made a mistake, that my entire dream was a farce. I contemplated returning to corporate America and asking for my old job back. Immediate doubts about my ability to be a businessman entered my mind. That lingering sentiment that I had made a terrible decision haunted my every thought. I was sopping in self-pity.

This was one of the toughest mental battles I ever had to endure as a young entrepreneur, even to this day. I made the battle ten times harder than it had to be, not only because I made poor decisions about Costa Rica but also because I hadn't anticipated the hit.

I lacked the wisdom at the time to know that when you decide to pursue your goals and dreams, something is bound to happen—something that will determine how much you really want it. Something will lead either to your breakdown or to your breakthrough. Something will require you to stretch and grow. Something you can choose to be bitter about or use to become better, smarter, and more focused.

This time was also a defining moment in my entrepreneurial career because I decided to stick it out. I chose not to run back to the comfort of having a job again. Somewhere inside, I regained that spark that had given me the courage to walk away from a flourishing career. I knew I had learned a valuable lesson.

Without a doubt, I still look back on that experience, confident that leaving corporate America to pursue my passion was the best choice I could have made. From that one decision—not giving up on my dream—I learned:

- How to deal with adversity
- How to take a loss and keep pushing forward
- How important it is to anticipate the hits so they don't permanently defeat you

Things aren't always going to go according to your plans. Life will always—*always*—hit you with something you didn't see coming. Anticipating the hits in life is simply a state of mind. You basically accept that overcoming challenges is a part of life. And when life calls your number and presents you with an unexpected challenge, you don't give up—you embrace it and fight your way through it. You don't blame circumstances or throw a never-ending pity party. You use your energy to persevere and come through the situation a better person.

Anticipating the hit does not exempt you from getting hit or even mean that the unexpected hits in life will hurt any less. It does mean a faster mental recovery time and that you won't allow yourself to be taken out by life's painful surprises.

The next time life hits you with a completely unexpected challenge, you can look life squarely in the eyes and say, "I was expecting you."

PRACTICING THE PRINCIPLE

> *It has been my philosophy of life that difficulties vanish when faced boldly.*
>
> Isaac Asimov

There is no physical training for the time an unanticipated hit flies in our direction. All of our preparation involves being mentally aware of one fact: Unexpected hits will come in our direction.

How do we mentally prepare ourselves to master the unexpected? There are several steps we can take in preparation of any hit that comes our way. This is a great section to refer back to in the future when you experience one of those setbacks.

Here are some ideas to make your deflated feeling go away so you can rebound quicker:

1. Accept that you can't stop undesirable things from happening, but you can control your response to them. Mental attitude is always important, never more than when it comes to dealing with negative responses and emotions.

   I completely delayed my recovery from the Costa Rica investment because I dwelled on everything that went wrong in the process. In my mind, I kept replaying everything leading up to the final phone call in which I learned I'd lost my entire investment. The reality is that I couldn't have done anything to prevent it from happening the way it did. My focus should have been on how I was going to respond. Unfortunately, it took me some time to realize this.

2. Think about everything you have to be grateful for and how much that outweighs what is against you now.

   No matter how big your mistake or what happens to tear you down, you must remember to be grateful for the simple things. It may be your friends, family, children, good health, a roof over your head, or the ability to simply take your next breath. Focus on the feelings that arise from gratitude, and it's sure to bring things back into perspective. This will allow you to generate positive thoughts during difficult moments.

   When I was beating myself up about my financial loss

in Costa Rica, I had so many other things to be grateful for—but I failed to focus on them. Gratitude could have helped put things in perspective and significantly reduce my recovery time.

3. Look for the lessons to be learned and draw something positive from them. Someone with great wisdom once said, "When you lose, don't lose the lesson."

Although I had taken a financial loss on the Costa Rica investment, I learned some valuable lessons that I still apply to this day when I experience significant setbacks. The lessons I learned were costly, but they would have cost me considerably more if I had not learned anything from the experience.

4. Have courage. Maya Angelou said it best when she wrote, "Courage is the most important of all the virtues because without courage, you can't practice any other virtue consistently." The best habits and qualities for showing up truly take practice. Find the courage to stand up regardless of what has knocked you down.

At some point, you must have the courage to stand in the midst of your trial and turn your situation around. It took me some time, but I finally got over my pity party, pushed past my fears, and gained enough courage to resume moving forward. In fact, I did not have to run back to the security of the career I had just left.

5. Don't forget that you are human. No human is perfect or has a life that runs smoothly for them at all times. Experiencing adversity brings greater appreciation for what is good. Learning lessons, even the hard ones, gives us more knowledge than if life simply let us pass through each experience without any challenges.

I have learned my greatest lessons not from my triumphs but from my trials. I carry that awareness with me every day as a reminder that I am resilient enough to make it through the most challenging situations.

ANTICIPATION IN MOTION

Anticipating the hits in life does not exempt you from getting hit, nor does it make it any less painful. Anticipation is a mindset to overcome anything that comes at you unexpectedly rather than allowing it to take you out. No one knows the mindset required to handle unexpected trials better than Aron Ralston. You may be familiar with his story.

Aron decided to go on a private hiking trip through the Blue John Canyon in Utah. He didn't bother telling anyone because he had only planned to be away for a couple of hours. At some point along the hiking trail, he decided to descend into one of the canyons—and the unexpected happened. An 800-pound boulder dislodged and fell into the canyon, pinning his crushed hand against the canyon wall. He knew immediately he was in trouble.

Since no one knew where he was, Aron knew no one would come searching for him. Five days later he was still there, his hand trapped between rock and wall, living off the little bit of water he had. When the water ran out, he drank his own urine. He rationed out the little bit of food he had as best he could. But now time was running out.

There was no way that he could have physically prepared for this unexpected blow in his life. However, he was able to tap into an incredibly powerful mindset. He wasn't going to let this situation take him out. Faced with no other choice, Aron did the unthinkable. He used a dull knife from his multi-tool set to amputate his own arm. How do you even mentally prepare to do such a thing? The alternative was dehydration and death.

Aron would not have been able to predict in a million years that life would put him in such a situation. Aron found great resolve at that moment. He wanted to live—and that's something only you can find within yourself when your hit comes.

Life seldom gives us a warning when we are going to receive one of those devastating blows. It's impossible to predict how we'll react when the blow happens. When life decides to call your number, you must reach into that place within yourself and access the strength that propels you to rise above your circumstance—

rather than allow yourself to die. It's not easy, but it's possible. It's a state of mind, and it's not just in Aron, it's also in you.

FIVE

TRUST THE PROCESS

" | *More important than the dream is the person you become in pursuit of the dream.*

| Les Brown

By now, you know that showing up for your life requires a clear purpose and a great deal of patience on your end. Equally important, you need to trust the process of showing up.

In the last chapter, we talked about how life is going to hit us with unexpected blows from time to time. Nothing we do can change that. All that is within our control prepares us mentally to handle the worst we may encounter and to choose our response carefully.

However, you can still do a great deal to change what lies ahead. Part of your power lies in learning to trust the process. Are you wondering what that means? Let me explain. In the midst of great uncertainty, pain, or misfortune, you have to trust that God will somehow work things out for your greater good. This requires faith. It's not the easiest thing to do, especially while you are experiencing a difficult and challenging time; which is, ironically, when you need it most.

In fact, trusting the process requires:

A great deal of faith. Very seldom is there physical evidence that any good will come from a struggle or a setback in life. We have to hold fast to an intangible belief in our hearts and minds that everything will work out for the best somewhere along the process.

Louis Moorer's life exemplifies trusting the process. Back on a sunny Saturday in 2003, Louis mounted his motorcycle as he'd done so many times before. He'd loved motorcycles since boyhood, and riding was always a great source of relaxation for him.

On this day, Louis made his way down the road, enjoying the sunshine and fresh air. He was riding to visit some relatives who lived nearby.

As Louis traveled the familiar two-lane road, an approaching car swerved into his lane. An experienced cyclist, Louis gripped the handlebars and made a sharp turn to the right, missing the car. But he wasn't out of danger yet.

Now Louis was moving too fast to navigate the tight curve right in front of him. He hit the curb, an impact that catapulted him off his motorcycle and into a raised brick flower bed by the roadside.

Still conscious, Louis struggled to stand, and succeeded—but at a horrific price. The movement pierced his spinal cord with a broken rib. He immediately collapsed again. Now there would be no getting back up.

Witnesses called for help, and an ambulance rushed to the scene. Paramedics stabilized Louis and loaded him into the ambulance. He needed emergency care as fast as possible.

Everything went black for Louis. When he came to, he lay in a hospital bed surrounded by family. He saw his mother staring down at him, emotional and concerned. Wanting to comfort her, Louis attempted to sit up and embrace his mother. He couldn't.

"You've been in a terrible accident, Louis," she said. "You must remain still. They're going to take you into immediate surgery."

In excruciating pain, Louis tried to respond. He really wasn't sure what the surgery was for, and he wanted answers as soon as it was over. As the anesthesia began to wear off, the doctor was called to his room. When the surgeon came through the door, Louis froze.

Can you immediately tell when someone has bad news for you just by the look on his face? It's a realization that usually knots your stomach. Louis saw that the doctor had that look.

The doctor glanced at Louis and then his family. The room was silent and everyone stared at the doctor, waiting to hear what he had to say. "I'm sorry, Louis. We did all we could in surgery, but your spinal injury is very severe."

Louis nodded his head. "Okay," he whispered.

The doctor continued talking. "You will most likely never walk again."

Never. That is one powerful word.

Imagine being only thirty years old and listening to your doctor tell you, in no uncertain terms, that you will likely never walk again. That meant Louis would never ride a motorcycle or do many of the things he'd enjoyed in life. He loved working out, playing sports, being an active guy—one who could never sit still and was always on the go.

At that moment, no one would have blamed Louis one bit if he lashed out or if he had become bitter and depressed over this sudden misfortune. Not a single person would have thought less of him if he indulged in self-pity or asked "Why me?" It would have been understandable, expected, and natural for most of us.

We so easily embrace faith when times are good and life seems to be working in our favor. Then something bad happens and everything changes. For some reason, people tend to abandon faith just when they need it most. We always need faith, but it's different to have faith on a great day than it is on a challenging day. Part of showing up for your life requires you to stop bitterness and anger from taking root. You must trust the process and believe that somehow, some way, God is going to guide your situation to a higher good.

It's with great joy I share that Louis didn't enter a state of depression or become bitter about his situation. He was wiser and more mature than many people twice his age when he made the conscious decision to show up for his life and commit to trusting the process. In the middle of a very tragic situation, Louis maintained a positive outlook that helped him decipher the truths in his life—at that moment, just as it was. He realized:

The doctor didn't necessarily have the final word on what the rest of his life would or would not be. He did!

For over a decade, Louis maintained a level of optimism, trusting the process on the most excruciating days. Does he have bad days? Yes. Do those bad days dictate his destiny, his mindset for the process? No! Through painstaking therapy, he has continued to mentally overcome the disappointment of countless failed treatments. When they don't work, he does not lose faith. While he gives his best to the process, he also finds strength in his faith every day. He trusts the process.

There is no doubt in my mind that if it wasn't for Louis's willingness to trust the process and not become a bitter soul in a continuous state of self-pity, he wouldn't have fared as well as he has. He wanted to defy the words of the doctor by trusting the process and putting in the work. This is how it played out for Louis:

- He was told that he would never walk again.
- He began to use a wheelchair.
- He progressed to a walker.
- Today, with great effort, Louis is able to walk with just the assistance of a cane.

Louis did, in fact, find the greater good in his misfortune. He happens to be one of my premier Inner Circle students, whom I have had the privilege of coaching on how to develop and deliver his story of triumph to benefit others.

Louis, the Comeback Expert, as we call him, now shares his amazing story on stage, inspiring audiences to make a comeback in their lives. Louis also continues to trust the process, believing that one day he will be able to walk with no assistance at all, in spite of what his doctor said. Guess what? I believe he is going to do it. If anyone can pull it off, it's Louis. He dreams of the day when he can walk into that doctor's office unassisted and show him how he defied the odds because he trusted the process.

GUIDED BY TRUST, FIRM IN FAITH

It sometimes seems repetitive to remind people that you need trust and faith to stay the course when things get rough. If you're headed into the eye of the hurricane, you need to believe that you will come out the other side. You'll even get the little reprieve in the center, that moment when you can recover your energy and find the strength to move forward. Before you know it, you'll make it through the storm, and it'll be smooth sailing ahead.

Some people may believe that faith is something you have when you are born. But that is not the case. Every single person in this world has the ability to trust the process and use faith to hold themselves to a higher standard—and a better result. Even a child understands this.

A child may be out on a playground swing, taking the biggest leap of faith possible—one that sends him sailing into the air until he lands on solid ground. Sometimes he misses the mark and may end up with a skinned knee or a broken arm. He grumbles, cries, and gets a cast, if one is required. Then he recovers and goes back out there and tries it again.

I am amazed at how much less fearful children are than adults, and how they always show their willingness to go through the process. They serve as a great example to all adults. Try pulling out your inner child and remembering that when bad things happen, it's not the end of the world. Go willingly through the process. Keep pushing forward.

One of the most memorable stories of trusting the process was shared by an unknown author. Honestly, every time I read this story I feel its message all over again. It's a brilliant reminder of the best way to approach life.

On a walk one day, a man came upon a cocoon. In one end, he saw the small opening where the transformed caterpillar, now a butterfly, struggled to free itself. Unable to take his eyes off this small miracle of nature in progress, he sat down and watched it unfold. It was long before video technology, so he could only record the scene in his mind, not for anyone else to see. It was his moment.

The butterfly struggled to squeeze through that small hole. For the longest time, it didn't give up. And then suddenly it did. It appeared that it could go no farther.

Unwilling to let the butterfly die in its cocoon, the man got up. He took a pair of scissors and snipped off the remaining bit of cocoon so the butterfly could be free to explore the world it was so eager to enter. Except the butterfly could not do that. Its body was swollen and its wings were small and shriveled, not able to spread open.

Setting the butterfly down as gently as he could, the man continued to watch it, waiting for that moment when the wings would expand and the butterfly would gracefully launch itself into the air. He waited. He continued to wait. Nothing happened. The wings didn't expand, and the body didn't contract.

The man was so sad. Suddenly he realized his desire to help had been a mistake. For a butterfly to fly, it must have that struggle with the small opening. It's how the fluid from the body of the butterfly is forced into the wings, ensuring it will be ready for flight.

After realizing what happened, the man understood a bit more about life. Struggles are a very important part of life. If we went through life without any obstacles, we would be crippled. We could not be as strong as we are, and we would never realize the power of faith. Just like the butterfly, we would never be able to take flight.

We all can become frustrated in the process and want to find a shortcut or a way to avoid the struggle. What we fail to realize in the process of struggle is that it prepares us to reach what we want to accomplish.

As this exemplifies, don't be so quick to resist the process. Don't try to avoid it. Instead, trust the process.

> **❝** *If you're still waiting for it, it means you're not ready for it ... whatever 'it' is ... so stop looking at waiting as a punishment and start looking at it as preparation.*
>
> Mandy Hale

As I mentioned earlier, trusting the process requires great patience, and a lack of patience is the reason most people struggle. You may believe that you were born impatient, but that's not necessarily true. It's a learned behavior and, therefore, a behavior that can be changed. Impatient people tend to get caught up in the opposition or delay of the moment, but they lose sight of future possibilities. There's a whole lot that goes on between what you are dealing with right now and what you intend to accomplish. Next time you find yourself being impatient, ask yourself this question: Why?

Take a hypothetical situation that most of us can relate to and then evaluate it.

- Do you think that extra minute in the checkout line is going to make your entire day unproductive? If so, the problem started way before you got to the store.

- Consider the possibility that there is a reason why you are there at that moment and not somewhere else. Is there a message for you on the cover of a magazine? Is there a long lost friend behind you in line? Do you need time to sort through something that's weighing on your mind?

- What else could have you frazzled? Is this your moment to take a breath and recharge your batteries so you can more easily trust in the process and make the most of the rest of your day?

Becoming aware of what we are feeling is an important part of trusting the process. The sooner we can connect with those emotions and understand why we're experiencing them, the more we can trust the process and the rewards it will bring.

PRACTICING THE PRINCIPLE

Learning to trust the process does not apply only when something devastating happens, as with Louis on his motorcycle. It applies to all challenges, large or small. Grasp this principle, and it will carry you far toward your ultimate goal of showing up.

The following set of practice steps requires you to invest time to do a little soul searching. But you will be glad you did—because the effort will pay off almost immediately by:

- Saving you time
- Giving you more energy
- Helping you remain focused and positive
- Unveiling your true potential
- Teaching you patience
- Acknowledging how much control you have

And of course,

- Guiding you to trust the process

The character-building rewards of trusting the process are phenomenal. They can make each and every one of us master of our destiny, once we understand that all things, good or bad, have a process. We define and control how our process goes for us because it all starts in the mind. How we perceive what happens to us, how we feel about it, and how we respond—none of these things has an objective reality. All are products of the mind. As the Bible says, "For as he thinketh in his heart, so is he." (Proverbs 23:7)

PRACTICE EXERCISE

It's time to grab some paper, find a place where you can let your thoughts flow, and dive into the details of learning to trust the process.

Here are the practice steps.

1. EVALUATE YOUR CURRENT SITUATIONS.

Summarize some of the challenges you currently face in your life. Make sure you include those you've set aside due to impatience or fear. Don't forget the ones you are struggling with, as well as the ones you are currently managing. Some of these challenges may include:

- Learning something new that will advance your career
- Overcoming a health issue by making healthier lifestyle choices
- Tapering impulsive or addictive behaviors
- Controlling emotional issues, such as anger or depression
- Procrastinating on completing a time-consuming project. It may be a project you fear, find dull or tedious, or one that tests your skills and strengths.
- Changing your behavior patterns in regard to how you think or act. Overcoming mental barriers is every bit as challenging as overcoming physical barriers. Mental barriers include:
  o Depression
  o Shyness
  o Lack of self-confidence
  o Anxiousness
  o Laziness
  o Negative talk
  o Excuse making

Now list everything in the order of importance to you. Start with what would lift the largest burden from your mind and free you from the mental jail that you may have placed yourself in by not trusting in the process. You'll be thankful you did.

_____

_____

_____

2. WRITE DOWN WHY YOU HAVE NOT COMMITTED FULLY TO THE PROCESS WITH THE CHALLENGE YOU PICKED FROM STEP ONE.

This statement may be a few sentences, a paragraph, or however long you need it to be. Be completely honest. Otherwise, it won't be an effective learning tool. Plus, being insincere is definitely not trusting the process. That's not you!

_____

_____

_____

3. LIST THE REASONS IT WILL BE BENEFICIAL FOR YOU TO TRUST THE PROCESS AND SEE THE CHALLENGE YOU PICKED THROUGH TO THE END.

Now you have the barriers out of the way, and you are focusing on the good that arises from trusting and committing to the process. Some motivating reasons to write this list are mentioned below, but don't be afraid to add more of your own. Think of the things that only you know about that are important and motivate you. Maybe it's being able to play a little longer with your kids without getting exhausted. Or perhaps you want to finish a grueling course of study to improve your chances of getting a promotion. You get the idea. You may wish to:

- Relieve stress and anxiety
- Have better health and more energy
- Gain more financial stability and freedom
- Have a happier and healthier relationship
- Gain peace of mind
- Experience achieving a hard-to-reach goal
- Learn that it's better to work the process than to work against it

_____

_____

4. IS THE CHALLENGE YOU CHOSE MEASURABLE?

Being able to measure your performance is a great help in trusting and making it through the process.

In Louis's case, his ultimate goal is to be able to walk without any assistance, but during a decade of going through the process, he has had plenty of measurable interim goals. His first was to make it out of the hospital bed into a wheelchair, then to take a few steps using a walker, next to walk without assistance using a walker, then to use only a quad cane, and after that to use a single cane as he does today. Now, it is to walk with no cane at all.

What kind of measurable milestones can you place throughout your process to keep you focused and moving forward? Write down the ways you can measure success against the challenge you chose to see through to completion.

_____

_____

_____

5. TAKING EVERYTHING YOU'VE LEARNED AND WRITTEN INTO ACCOUNT, CAN YOU SET A COMPLETION DATE?

There may very well be no end in sight for what you've chosen. If that's the case, acknowledge it and move on. If you can set a realistic end date, write it down. Of course, you can be aggressive with this if you are willing to give up other things to free more time for this process.

_____

_____

6. WHAT CAN YOU DO TO MAKE IT EASIER TO ENDURE AND TRUST THE PROCESS?

There are three areas to focus on for this step: attitude, action, and acceptance. If you can focus on these three areas, you will significantly increase your chances of making it through the process.

- List three ways you can adjust your attitude toward this particular challenge to provide a more positive outlook and increase your chances of actually making it through the process.

_____

_____

_____

- How we handle the process is based on our outlook. We must always be intentional about forming the right attitude.

- List three action steps you can take as you go through the process you are attempting to complete. These should be tangible things such as studying, physical exercise, or other steps that show you are committed to seeing things through.

Many people get stuck in the process or postpone completing it because they avoid taking action. You want to continue identifying action steps—and taking them—until you have overcome or completed your challenge.

_____

_____

_____

- List three things you must accept about the process in order to trust it. These will be things that are outside your control. It's a huge step in the right direction if you can accept things that are not in your control.

_____

_____

_____

Often, we get held up because we focus on things we can't control rather than simply accepting that what is happening is part of the process and moving forward. This is a mighty distraction from the things we _can_ control, which is where our efforts should be focused.

> ❝ | _God, grant me the serenity to accept the things I cannot change, the courage to change the things I can, and the wisdom to know the difference._
>
> | Reinhold Niebuhr

7. ENJOY AN AMAZING TRANSFORMATION!

The preceding steps may not seem as simple as others in this book. But once you understand how it feels, and you begin to see the benefits of trusting the process, you will find that it gets easier as you go along. You will understand what is required to move toward your goal. You'll be able to hold yourself accountable throughout the process. You'll gain an understanding of how much the process can mean to you and what a better person it helps you to become. You'll also learn how to convert your trials into triumphs.

THE PROCESS IN MOTION

The bamboo tree is a most remarkable plant. It doesn't grow like other trees. If you plant one, it's going to require some trust on your part. That's right, trust!

You first have to find good soil for the seed. After you have planted the seed, you have to pay close attention to it, watering it regularly to nurture it. Still, you won't see immediate results from your efforts. After a year of watering and nurturing the seed, the ground will still appear to be barren, showing no sign of a sprout. This makes it very challenging to trust the process. But you must resist the urge to give up, and continue to water the seed and take care of it.

After two years of watering and nurturing the seed, the ground will still appear to be barren. This is when your patience really becomes essential and when the average person typically abandons the process. Even after two additional years of diligently watering and nurturing the seed, you still won't see your bamboo tree break through the ground. By this point, you have put in four years of work, and you still don't see any results for your effort. There's no bamboo tree in sight. Not even a sprout.

If you have ever pursued a long-term goal for which you have been putting in consistent effort without noticeable results, you already know that the lack of visible results makes you really begin to question the process or even consider quitting. But just as in life, during the period in which the average person would have already quit caring for the bamboo seed, something amazing happens.

In the fifth year, the bamboo tree breaks through the ground. After all that time, the seed suddenly sprouts and grows at an accelerated rate. In a few weeks, the bamboo tree can grow up to ninety feet.

Often our goals and dreams grow in a similar way to the bamboo tree. Our dream represents the seed, and we have to water it and nurture it by putting in the time and effort to make it become a reality. We can go for weeks, months, and years without seeing the results we would like to see. The key is to trust the process and continue to do our part, watering and nurturing our goals and dreams—because in an *instant* things can turn around at a supernatural rate in your favor. Your business can suddenly come together and take off, your health can make a dramatic shift for the better, your relationship can go in a positive new direction, and your goals and dreams can suddenly become a reality.

None of those amazing transformations are possible if you allow yourself to get caught up judging the circumstances when things don't happen according to your timeline. In spite of what you see, you must maintain a spirit of faith.

Continue consistently doing the work.

And most importantly, trust the process.

SIX

BE UNSTOPPABLE

❝ *Life begins at the end of your comfort zone.*

Neale Donald Walsch

Have you ever resolved to do something and then discovered that some unforeseen obstacle was in your way? You started off thinking, "I can do this," and then all of a sudden, you began to think, "Maybe I can't do this." You've likely experienced that not only once but several times. At one point, all of us have fallen short of a goal or dream—not because it was unattainable or because we didn't have what it took to accomplish it, but because we just stopped.

When we stop doing something of significance to us, we usually follow it with a slew of justifications. We say things like:

- I didn't have the means to see it through.
- My circumstances changed.
- It was harder than I anticipated. *This one is thought silently more than spoken aloud.*

Every justification we can come up with equates to one thing—we stopped short of our goal. Eloquent excuses are no better than fumbling over words when trying to justify a shortfall. An excuse is an excuse, no matter how we try to dress it up. It has been said that you can put lipstick on a pig; but guess what, it's still a pig. Likewise, you can make an excuse sound really compelling—but it is still an excuse. That is a tough pill for many people to swallow, especially when they know they didn't put everything they had into the effort. They could have pushed themselves a little further. They did not offer their best selves to the process.

> " *All you can do is all you can do, but all you can do is enough. However, make sure you do all you can do.*
>
> ## A. L. Williams

Billionaire insurance mogul A. L. Williams nailed it on the head when he said, "All you can do is all you can do, but all you can do is enough. However, make sure you do all you can do." When you know in your heart that you've done all you can do to accomplish your goal, including exhausting all your options, effort, and resources, it truly is enough. How many of us can look at ourselves in the mirror and reflect back on a time when we fell short and honestly said that we did absolutely all that we could do?

To be unstoppable, you have to venture outside your comfort zone and realize that your potential is greater than your natural state of comfort allows it to be.

There are three things that I believe we should all strive to be:

- *Uncomfortable:* Do not put up comfort boundaries that stop growth and stunt your innate ability to be unstoppable.

- *Unrealistic:* Many dreams are stopped dead in their tracks because someone wanted to remain realistic. We still benefit from some really amazing dreams that were labeled unrealistic and became a reality. Thomas Edison famously tried ten thousand different substances for the filament in his light bulb but none worked for more than a few hours. He said, "I have not failed. I have found ten thousand ways that will not work." He eventually discovered a carbonized bamboo filament that lasted up to twelve hundred hours—and created the electrified modern world. Being realistic is overrated. Never shoot down the ideas inside of you that demand attention because others cannot latch onto your dream or vision. The dream was given to you, and it's yours to protect and cultivate, even when it seems unrealistic to the naysayers.

- *Unstoppable:* Work your plan and plan to work. No matter what obstacles come your way, resolve that you will not quit. You may have to slow down, or you may even get discouraged during the pursuit, but quitting is not an option. Stopping short of your dream is not an option. Here's another bit of wisdom from Edison, a man who never quit: "Many of life's failures are people who did not realize how close they were to success when they gave up."

The combination of these three principles is so powerful when it comes to pursuing your aspirations. It's the blend that gives you the fuel and drive to reach goals, achieve big dreams, and make incredible things happen. Never settle for less than being uncomfortable, unrealistic, and unstoppable. Nothing significant happens for you when you remain in your comfort zone, where you will rarely push yourself to the limit. As a result, you will stop short of your dreams.

When you decide to show up for your life, it means that you have made the decision to be unstoppable. It means that when obstacles are presented, you will find a way to go around them, over them, under them, or break right through them. Your mental toughness is at its best. Is being unstoppable easy? No, it isn't—but it is necessary if you want to live an extraordinary life.

I've always enjoyed being a coach. I love helping individuals and corporations strategically craft and deliver their stories to increase sales, influence and produce better personal and business results. At one point, I also coached and mentored people in a particular real estate investment niche that I have had success with since leaving corporate America. To this day, outside of my speaking and mentoring business, I actively invest in real estate. It's something that I believe strongly in and enjoy pursuing, having learned some valuable lessons and having increased my real estate knowledge. My Costa Rica mishap was my early lesson in anticipating the hits and being unstoppable in the pursuit of my goals and dreams.

Years ago, when I was coaching students on how to invest in real estate, there was a young man named Freppel who approached me about coaching during a real estate investor networking meeting. We were about five minutes into our conversation when I realized that Freppel would not be able to enroll in my coaching program because he didn't have the money to invest in it. I thought he was a pretty nice guy, so I gave him my telephone number to allow him to call for advice until he could actually enroll in the program.

Over the course of the next few months, Freppel called me once or twice a week. Every time we spoke on the phone, I discovered he faced an additional challenge or obstacle. Yes, inadequate funds were one challenge, but it was not the only one. I invited him to an investor networking meeting that would offer some information I believed would benefit him—only to discover that he didn't have a vehicle. It's pretty hard to get around and inspect investment properties without a vehicle to get you there. That was something else he was going to have to address.

During another conversation, I shared a resourceful website with him and told him to pull it up while I was on the phone with him—only to discover that he didn't own a computer, and he didn't have Internet access at his house. Another problem. This guy was clearly at a disadvantage. You can be creative in real estate and position yourself to make money even if you don't have funds available yourself, but I don't think I have ever seen that happen without a car or computer access. I had to make sure that I wasn't wasting my time by helping him. There's only so much you can do to assist someone who doesn't have the basic tools necessary for the job.

I said, "Freppel, how are you going to search for properties on the Internet and go look at them if you don't have a car or Internet access on a computer at your house?"

Freppel replied, "I have a bicycle and I plan on looking at properties that are within an hour's ride of my house."

I chuckled, wondering how he was going to search for properties on the Internet.

Freppel wasn't bothered by my chuckle and answered immediately and honestly. "There is a public library within a twenty-minute bike ride of my house, and if you wait long enough in the Internet access computer lab, one of computers becomes available."

Part of me admired Freppel's determination, but I don't mind confessing I was thinking this guy has to be crazy because this is completely unrealistic. There are plenty of wannabe investors in this world who have the resources, the basic knowledge, a car, and a computer with Internet access. These aspiring investors still have a very difficult time landing a real estate deal. Yet Freppel planned to land one without even the most basic resources at his disposal? His ambition was off the charts, and the prospect of achievement seemed unrealistic.

For the next couple of months, Freppel called periodically with questions about various aspects of the business. I helped him as best I could and always ended the call with the same question. "Do you have a car or the Internet at home yet?"

"No, Andy. I am still using my bike and the public library." I would hang up my phone at a loss for words and shake my head in disbelief. He'd lasted longer than a lot of people who had the resources to make real estate investing work.

For the next month, I did not hear from Freppel at all, and I thought he might have finally realized his limitations were too big to conquer and given up. Then one day he called me, and I could hear the excitement in his voice. He said, "I found a deal."

"Freppel, are you sure you found a deal?" I tried to conceal my shock.

"Yes, for the past couple of months, I have been riding my bike to the public library and waiting patiently for a computer to become available. Once I got on the computer, I used all the websites that you gave me to possibly locate real estate deals. When I found something that could potentially be a deal, I rode my bike to go and take a look at the property. Sometimes, it would take an hour each way. But no matter how discouraged I got, I never stopped. And I finally found a deal."

I was in total disbelief and needed to verify this myself. I arranged to meet with Freppel, who convinced me that he did, in fact, do everything I had told him to do to locate a distressed property that was for sale by the owner. He used the very contract I had provided him to get the owner's commitment. As I had promised him when we first met, I put up the deposit for him on the house.

During his inspection period, he secured a second buyer who was willing to pay him more than what he had it under contract for. Sparing you the real estate jargon, he essentially bought the house, which I funded for him, and resold it the same day of his closing to another investor without doing any repairs to the house and made $8,000 on his first real estate deal.

Freppel had no funds of his own, no vehicle, and no computer with Internet access at home. What he did have was an unstoppable spirit. Because I assisted him, he thought I was some kind of a hero. But he was the real hero. He was the victor of his own life, not falling victim to the fact that he didn't have certain tools. He had determination and desire, combined with a commitment to make it all happen.

Freppel embodies all of the principles in this book, but it was his consistent effort to be unstoppable that enabled him to achieve his goals. He faced obstacles, but he knew they were surmountable with the right no-quit attitude.

Too often we stop in the pursuit of our goals and dreams, convinced that we lack the necessary tools, contacts, education, talent, or capital. Yet, we often have everything we need, as long as we are willing to be unstoppable.

SHOW THE WORLD WHAT YOU'VE GOT

> *It's not what you don't have, but it is what you think you need that keeps you from having success in life.*
>
> ## Les Brown

As you look at your life and think about your goals, dreams, and the things you are hoping to accomplish, how do you feel about them? Are you willing to share them with others? If you have already shared them, how have others responded to you? Do they look at you as if you're crazy?

You know that look. Someone can look at you without saying a word and yet tell you what they're thinking just by their eyes and the expression on their face. They might as well say, "You must be crazy. Get your head out of the clouds."

If you have never gotten that look, there is a great chance that you're not dreaming big enough. That's right.

You should expect to hear people say:

- "Be more realistic."
- "You're crazy."
- "Do you really think you can do that?"

The only way you can truly do something extraordinary in your life is to dream about what intimidates you and seems almost impossible. Dream the type of dream that you look at and ask yourself, "How in the world am I going to do this?" Dexter Yager said, "If a dream is big enough, then the odds don't matter."

Other people's opinions about your dream are entirely secondary to your own personal belief. You have the ability to nurture, plan, act upon, and ultimately fulfill that dream in spite of the doubters. Don't downsize your dream in response to naysayers. Those people do not have power over your actions—unless you hand it to them.

Long-distance swimmer Diana Nyad knows what it means

to be unstoppable. Decades ago, Diana had the inconceivable dream of swimming from Cuba to Florida. In her first attempt in 1978, at the age of twenty-eight, she failed to complete the 110-mile swim from Havana to Key West. Most people believed that since she was in her prime—young, strong, and superbly conditioned—it was then or never.

Diana didn't agree with most people. Thirty-three years after her first attempt in 1978, Diana decided it was time to try again. She had come close to letting her dream die, but now she had decided to reignite it—and this time, without a shark cage. She organized a support team and prepared as hard has she could for the enormous challenge. In August 2011, she attempted the swim again. Once more, she had to abandon her efforts. This time, it was the strong currents and winds that stopped her.

The following month, September 2011, Diana made a third try—falling short again. This time, it was poisonous jellyfish stings. Those jellyfish may have stopped her that day, but they didn't stop the dream from being alive and well inside Diana's heart and mind.

The fourth attempt ended barely after it began in August 2012. Nyad swam into storms and jellyfish almost immediately.

Would it ever happen? Could a dream that she'd had since before her first attempt in 1978 ever come to fruition? She had proven her willingness, shown her determination, and demonstrated her physical strength. But she had been defeated by the elements four times.

The day for attempt number five arrived on August 31, 2013, with sixty-four-year-old Diana Nyad leaving the shoreline of Cuba. This time, the currents were with her, and she wore a new wet suit and breathing mask to protect against venomous jellyfish. After fifty-three strenuous hours, never leaving the water, never even holding on to the side of the boat, she stumbled onto the beach at Key West, Florida.

Her failed attempts had received minor media attention but her successful venture was reported all over the world. At the age of sixty-four, she was the first person to successfully complete the swim from Cuba to Florida without the use of a shark cage.

I watched as Diana was interviewed by one of the national television stations. She had just been released from the hospital, where doctors restored her fluids and made sure she was still healthy after the grueling feat. Her face was weather-beaten, and she could barely talk with her lips and tongue so swollen by the salty ocean water. The news correspondent recapped her gut-wrenching first four failed attempts, and the unbelievable extremes she demanded of her body and mind during the successful fifth attempt. With genuine curiosity, the correspondent asked, "What was different this time? How in the world were you able to pull this off at the age of sixty-four, when you failed at the age of twenty-eight and the four previous attempts?"

Diana explained that she had used a mantra this time. When her body was fatigued, when her lips and throat were burning from the lacerations and salty ocean water, when her mind began to waver, she repeated to herself, "Find a way." Those three words helped to achieve a goal she had pursued for nearly thirty-five years.

Find a way.

To be unstoppable and show up for your life, you have to embody Diana's mantra. You must find a way and not allow any circumstances to divert your attention or distract your desire. You have to be willing to do everything humanly possible to keep pushing toward your goal. You can't let anything stop you from realizing your dream.

PRACTICING THE PRINCIPLE

> " *Tough times never last, but tough people do.*
>
> Robert Schuller

Leslie Calvin Brown, also known as my mentor Les Brown, told me and many of his audiences something very powerful that demonstrates the heart and mind of someone who is unstoppable.

He said, "*If you want a thing bad enough to go out and fight for it, to work day and night for it, to give up your time, your peace and sleep for it, if all that you dream and scheme is about it, and life seems useless and worthless without it, if you gladly sweat for it and fret for it and plan for it and lose all your terror of the opposition for it, if you simply go after that thing you want with all of your capacity, strength and sagacity, faith, hope and confidence and stern pertinacity, if neither cold, poverty, famine, nor gout, sickness nor pain, of body and brain, can keep you away from that thing that you want, if dogged and grim you beseech and beset it, with the help of God, you will get it!*"

Why is that motivational statement so true? Because we all have the capacity at any given moment to impose our will and resolve to be unstoppable in the pursuit of our goals and dreams.

It's time to believe it.

It's time to become unstoppable.

ANALYZING YOUR WILLINGNESS

This is the time to look at your life and think about what is required to make your dream, the thing you want so badly, become a reality. In this section, we will go through a series of questions to determine if you're truly working your plan for your goals and dreams—or if you are simply going through the motions.

WARNING: This exercise may require you to get uncomfortable. You may even come up with ideas that seem unrealistic. To ensure your ultimate success, you will have to be unstoppable.

STEP ONE: WHAT IS THE ONE BURNING DESIRE THAT YOU MUST FULFILL?

Turn over the dormant rocks that your dreams, goals, and visions have been hiding under in your mind. Mix things up any way you can to release your true desires. Find the one that speaks to you most and commit to pursuing it. Say it, write it down, and make it crystal clear in your mind. Find your purpose.

_____

_____

STEP TWO: SET THE FRAMEWORK.

Think about what is required for you to make your dream happen. Ask yourself the following questions:

1. *Have I worked on this goal at all?* Determine if you've begun to lay the foundation for pursuing your greatest desire. Think about the skills you have in place and those you need to develop.

_____

_____

_____

2. *Have I already started the process?* Although your burning passion may have been in the back of your mind until attempting this exercise, think about what you may have been doing that could help the process. Is there anything you are currently doing, or do you already have any skills that could contribute to your goal?

_____

_____

_____

3. *If you quit pursuing your passion in the past, why?* Most people have given up on what they truly wanted at some point. They resorted to excuses to justify quitting. Think about what excuses you've used in the past and commit to not using them anymore. Creating excuses is one of the most counterproductive things you can do. Excuses make you shrink. They will never allow you to grow.

_____

_____

_____

4. *Am I committed to accomplishing this goal?* **Many things sound fantastic and adventurous when we think about them. We may even get all excited when we envision a goal or talk about it with friends and family. But if our actions do not support our enthusiasm, it is one of the surest signs that we lack commitment. Any goal worth attaining is going to require true commitment. One of the best definitions that I have ever heard about commitment came from personal development trainer George Zalucki. He said, "Commitment is doing the thing you said you would do, long after the mood you said it in has left you."**

_____

_____

_____

STEP THREE: CREATE THE PLAN.

Consider the things you can begin doing every day, starting today, to become unstoppable in the pursuit of what you desire. Here's a small layout that is simple to follow and implement. Not every day will be easy, so don't trick yourself into thinking so. But every day will be rewarding, and you'll know you are that much closer to becoming unstoppable.

- *Create a one-day goal.* This is your goal for today. It is the start of the journey, a time to think outside the box and explore any and all opportunities that pop into your head. You can do this by:

  o Reading

  o Researching

  o Listening to motivational audio books or speeches

  o Seeking something or someone who inspires you

  o Writing down strong visualizations of yourself accomplishing a future goal

When you have completed this goal, you will have either a strong mental image of what you see happening in your future or indisputable written evidence that you've started the journey. The process may start off a little slower than you would like, but in time, you will pick up momentum.

- *Create weekly goals.* This is your weekly blueprint for success. Use it to structure your week to accomplish specific tasks. Short of something absolutely unavoidable, allow no excuses to divert you from your weekly goals. This will give you direction during the week and, ultimately, more confidence, energy, focus, and a greater sense of commitment.

  o When you are putting together your weekly goals, give yourself a fresh start of a full day by beginning it tomorrow. But do not delay by allowing yourself to wait until Monday—unless, of course, tomorrow is Monday!

  o Build on what you accomplish each day so you can see active progression throughout the week. This will give you a greater sense of accomplishment at the end of the week and allow you to build momentum. If research is involved, don't allow yourself to become stagnant or get stuck in analysis paralysis. Learn the essentials and move to action. You can always continue to learn in the process.

- *Create monthly goals.* These will be an accumulation of your weekly goals. You should allot yourself time to evaluate and modify anything that has proven to be ineffective. There is no sense stressing yourself by holding on to an approach that is not working for you. Accept that you've learned something valuable, make the appropriate adjustments, and keep pushing forward.

- *Create quarterly goals.* These are your combined monthly goals, but they cause you to look further down the road.

Remember, when you are setting all of these goals, be as specific as possible. Set measurable goals so you can track your progress and give yourself a timeframe to hold yourself accountable for getting things done. Most worthy goals are going to take time to accomplish. They are certainly unlikely to take place overnight, so be patient yet persistent.

Also remember that you need to be consistent. It's important to develop the habit of setting daily, weekly, monthly, and quarterly goals. You'll be surprised at how the consistent act of setting your goals will give you momentum in the ultimate pursuit of what you desire. This is the type of momentum that helps you to become unstoppable.

If you take the time to do the exercises above and commit to following the steps consistently, you'll be well on your way to accomplishing what you ultimately desire. The key is to remember there will be challenges along the way. Everyone has them, including you. The difference between those who make it through the challenge and those who fall short is an unstoppable spirit and the willingness to persist, no matter what.

UNSTOPPABLE IN MOTION

" *Your mind is capable of making all things real for you ... and with positive thinking and a tight plan, you can become unstoppable!*

Markesa Yeager

My friend, Pauline Victoria Aughe, truly represents what it means to be unstoppable. I met Pauline years ago at a speaker training conference. She immediately caught my attention because she has no arms or legs. But you couldn't miss how she radiated happiness through her beautiful smile and amazing spirit.

As our training event went on, I was blown away to learn that Pauline had come all the way from her home in Hawaii to attend the event. The distance and the challenges she must have faced on that long trip astounded me. That would only be the first way she amazed me throughout the weekend.

She also did things that I didn't expect her to have the ability to do. I remember watching Pauline take copious notes all weekend. She actually did that by holding a pen between her chin and shoulder and bending over until the pen touched the paper. She maneuvered her entire upper body on every pen stroke. Even so, her handwriting was far better than average.

Perhaps the most memorable moment was watching Pauline being interviewed by one of the training facilitators. It was a training exercise designed to give some insight into Pauline's life while demonstrating the process for extracting someone's signature story.

Pauline was asked to name her biggest challenge in life. Every one of us thought that the answer would be obvious—she had no arms and legs. Pauline gazed up and pondered the question. She then looked at the interviewer and said, "I don't know. I can't really think of any at the moment." All of us in the room immediately got goose bumps on our arms. Some even began to cry because we knew that she was being absolutely sincere in her response. In that moment of revelation from Pauline, all our personal problems were suddenly slammed into perspective.

People like Pauline do not focus on their limitations. From birth she has been unstoppable, overcoming the inconceivable challenges that came with being born without limbs. Today, Pauline is an author, inspirational speaker, and a blogger. She even created a series of videos to physically demonstrate how she does such amazing things, to inspire others to push pass their limitations.

She hasn't allowed her disability to stop her. She cooks for herself, drives on her own in a modified vehicle, and types more than thirty words per minute using a stick that she holds between her chin and shoulder. Pauline is married and gave birth to a healthy son. She's done all the things others may think would be impossible if they viewed her situation only from the outside. But she never even considered what others thought impossible. She did what she wanted.

When you decide to show up for your life, be like Pauline. She is a true example of what it means to be unstoppable.

SEVEN

HAVE FAITH

> **❝** *Now faith is the substance of things hoped for, the evidence of things not seen.*
>
> Hebrews 11:1

Difficult life challenges can seem like mountains. No matter how hard we try, they just don't budge. Over time, the frustrations pile up, and we become discouraged—making the battle all the more difficult. We begin to ask ourselves, "What am I going to do? How am I going to make it through this?"

There's a natural inclination for us to feel overwhelmed in those moments, to feel trapped as we become increasingly more consumed with worry, fear, and doubt. To make matters worse, there often appears to be no solution within grasp or sight. Only one approach works in these types of situations.

We have to turn to faith. Faith is an essential principle if you want to show up for your life. Faith is the belief that God has a purpose and a plan for your life, even when your circumstances seem to be saying the exact opposite. Now I have my concept of God, and you may have another. Nevertheless, the power idea here is faith.

We find it easy to express some level of faith when things are working in our favor and life is looking promising. In those moments, it's not difficult to have a positive outlook. But life has a way of shaking things up and putting us in difficult circumstances when we least expect it. That's when the real test begins. We have to find a way to maintain a level of faith that will take us through the difficult times, even if the future shows no signs of getting better.

Sometimes we can only make it through those difficult moments by drawing from the hope that things will get better. Such hope cannot exist without some degree of faith. Therefore, faith is one of the single most important elements to showing up in all circumstances. No matter how hard life may be or how much uncertainty exists, we must trust and believe that there is light at the end of the tunnel. Often the only light you will find is your faith.

Years ago, I attended a weekend speaker training designed to help attendees craft and deliver their personal stories. You may notice that in addition to facilitating, I have attended, and continue to attend, many personal development and training events myself. I don't plan to ever stop, as I believe it is essential for continual growth. There were about one hundred people present at this particular event, and we were assigned to groups of ten participants each. We did several exercises during the day that required us to deliver one- to three-minute speeches in front of the attendees at our table.

One guy at our table was full of so much passion that every time he got up to speak, you could feel his conviction down to your core. He had married the love of his life, but she had been diagnosed with cancer. He loved her so much and wanted to ensure that she got the absolute best care possible. Not wanting to leave her well-being in anyone else's hands, he quit his job and lived off his savings to become her caregiver.

This man was incredible. He took care of his wife every single moment until she finally passed away. Now that she was gone, he was adamant about keeping her legacy alive. He started a foundation in her name to encourage and support cancer patients and their caregivers. Cancer is already an emotional subject before you consider the idea of helping those who are affected by it. This man's story made it even more emotional. Every time he spoke, his eyes watered, his voice filled with emotion, and he transferred his passion to all of us. We could not help being moved by this man's powerful message and delivery. And all of this took place in just the first day.

That first day of training was very intense, with only two breaks—one for lunch and one for dinner. I thought it was odd that this man who was so passionate and working so hard during the training chose not to eat anything. Later in the evening, after I put away my training materials in my room, I decided to explore the hotel. I thought it would be great to move around since we'd been confined to a single room for the entire day.

I headed down to the lobby, where I saw that same passionate man sitting with his luggage. I decided to swing by and strike up a conversation. I let him know how impressed I had been by his story and how it had touched me on a personal level. We spoke for a few minutes, and then I continued my tour of the hotel.

I spent about forty-five minutes walking around and, when I got back to the lobby, I thought it was bizarre that he was still sitting there with his luggage. I waved, got on the elevator, and headed back up to my room. But I couldn't get the man's image out of my mind. Something inside of me was telling me to head back down to the lobby and check on him.

Back in the lobby for the second time, I approached the guy, and we started chatting. A few minutes into the conversation, I finally had to ask, "Why do you still have your luggage with you? Why not take it to your room?"

He said softly, "Actually, I don't have a room."

"Why don't you have a room? Are all the rooms full?" I asked.

He shook his head no and said, "When I heard about this training, I absolutely knew that I needed to be here and as you know, I am extremely passionate about this nonprofit organization that I am starting. Learning how to share my story and the mission of my nonprofit is going to be crucial for getting funding and making an impact. So I decided to take a step of faith, and I literally used every penny that I had to my name to book my flight and register for this event. Based on the first day of training alone, I'd say it was worth it."

I thought maybe that was why he skipped both lunch and dinner.

I said to him, "Let me get this straight, you used all of your money to book your flight and register for this training?"

"Yes," he replied with absolute conviction and a smile on his face.

"So are you saying that you don't have a hotel room and haven't even figured out where you are sleeping during this weekend?"

His smile didn't waver and he looked at me, very content with the situation that many would find distressing, and said, "You got it."

"Well, have you figured out where you are staying yet?" I asked.

"No," he replied.

I couldn't believe this. "What are you going to do? I would be stressed out if I were you."

He said, "I am not worried about it. I needed to be here, and I know that everything will work out. It always does." I thought to myself, this guy is either crazy or has extraordinary faith.

"Is there anything I can do to assist you?" I asked.

"No, I'm fine. Everything will work out," he insisted.

"Well, I wish you luck then," I said. I turned away in complete disbelief and headed back up to my room. His words and story were playing out in my mind. I honestly couldn't believe that he would spend his last bit of money to come to the training and not even know where he was going to sleep. All day during the training he had been completely present and engaged in all the exercises and activities. No one would have ever known that he spent all he had to get to that conference. Nor would anyone have guessed in a million years that he didn't even know where he would be sleeping over the weekend.

At that point, I knew I had to do something. I picked up the room telephone and called down to the front desk. I asked if they could transfer me from my current room, which had one king size bed, to a room with two queen size beds. They said it wouldn't be a problem and, shortly after, they sent someone up to help with my luggage and to give me my new room keys.

Okay, I was all situated. I had a room with two queen beds and plenty of space. It was time to make the journey down to the lobby again. I stood in that elevator and when the door chimed and opened, I was not surprised to find that man still sitting there, looking calm and content as could be.

I walked directly to him and said, "I know that you said that you are fine. But I happen to have an extra queen bed in my room, and you are more than welcome to stay there for the weekend."

He asked, "Are you sure?"

"Absolutely." I had no hesitation whatsoever.

He stood up, looked me in the eye, and said, "Thank you so much. I truly appreciate you doing this for me. This training event is such an important part of what I need to do to honor my deceased wife and carry out the mission of my nonprofit. I couldn't have afforded to miss it even though I didn't know how I was going to make it through the weekend."

I said, "Well, it worked out, just like you knew it would." As we walked off, I marveled at this man's faith and couldn't help but reflect on what I would do in such a situation. Would I be able to demonstrate faith the way he had?

> *Faith is taking the first step even when you don't see the whole staircase.*
>
> Martin Luther King, Jr.

Aside from an exceptional training seminar, that weekend provided one of the most valuable lessons in my life. Witnessing that man's faith, conviction, and passion was incredible. I learned that faith gets rewarded and that, often, when we are in pursuit of our goals and dreams, there are going to be moments of uncertainty and doubt. In those moments, we need to trust God and move forward in faith.

Finding the courage to commit to your dreams is easier with faith because it is not all based on your efforts alone. Your dreams may not unfold on your own timetable or in the way you want, but the path will show itself in due time. Looking back, I realize that helping this man had nothing to do with me. I was simply a tool used by God to reward his faith.

For the rest of the training weekend, I watched this man have several breakthroughs of his own. He made some powerful connections, all of which took his vision and his nonprofit organization to new heights. The reason these things were possible was because he had the willingness to take a major step of faith toward his dream.

Had he not exercised faith and allowed fear and worry to take root instead, he might have postponed his dream and missed out on a life-changing experience.

And guess what?

So would I.

LIVING A FAITH-BASED LIFE

> *Faith isn't faith until it's all you're holding on to.*
>
> ## Patrick Overton

No person is immune to moments of doubt, especially in times of fear and worry. Doubt is a part of the human experience. It still comes, even when you have faith. In those moments, the circumstances can make it seem as if our dreams cannot possibly come true.

Doubt is often attached to:

- Financial pressures
- Health issues
- Relationship challenges
- Significant losses

In those moments, sometimes the only thing you can draw from to keep pushing forward, the one and only thing that gives you strength to stay in the game, is your faith. You have to hold on to faith with all you have and never surrender it, no matter what.

Through my life experiences, I have seen and learned firsthand how faith is key to keeping our dreams alive. I'm not saying faith always comes easily, but I have noted how it has affected my life in the most amazing ways.

Without it, I never would have had the opportunity to impact thousands of lives across the world as a motivational speaker and coach. I certainly couldn't have written this book, if I had not taken that step of faith back in 2004 when I left corporate America. Do you know how long I agonized over making that decision? I worried about leaving my consistent biweekly paycheck for the uncertainty of becoming an entrepreneur. I wondered what people would think about me trading in stability by leaving the career I had spent more than five college years preparing to launch. I feared failure and the potential shame of having to ask for my job back if things didn't work out. There were so many doubts, and there was so much to fear.

Ultimately, my faith gave me the courage to resign and pursue what was in my heart.

When you act from a place of faith, you release the fear, worry, and doubt. You stop thinking about what you don't want, and focus clearly on what you do want. You stop focusing on your limitations. Instead, you focus on the possibilities.

My life, both personally and professionally, would not be what it is today had I not acted from a place of faith. You have the opportunity to do the same at any moment and in any situation. No one, aside from you, can decide to abandon your fear, worry, and doubt. Only you can latch on to faith and take action toward your dreams.

I would be misleading you if I allowed you to think it was possible to show up for your life without exercising faith. Faith is essential to creating an extraordinary life. You can operate from a place of faith on a daily basis. All you have to do is make that choice.

Every single person has the ability to tap into their faith—once you do, there is no shortage of it.

You can never run out of faith. You can only run away from it.

PRACTICING THE PRINCIPLE

> *You can do anything you want in life, even the things that seem impossible. The only one stopping you is yourself! Keep your faith and you will find a way.*
>
> Hussein Nishah

There is no real way to teach a person how to have faith, but there is a way to demonstrate what faith isn't. There is even a way to show how not having it creates unnecessary struggle and worry. Unlike the other ways that you have practiced the principles in this book, this section is going to be a reflection on what happens when you fail to exercise your faith—you know, those moments you are consumed with fear and worry and fail to act. When that happens, you may find yourself paralyzed to the point of delaying your goals and dreams. Yet when faith is allowed to play itself out, you always manage to find the solution. You gain clarity, and you're now equipped to overcome even the most daunting challenges.

Let's take some time for you to recall a situation from your past in which you were so filled with fear, doubt, and worry that it drained your energy. It made you want to take a long nap and wake up when the situation was over. That is where your first lesson will be learned. Find a quiet place or take a walk, or whatever quiets your mind, and ponder the following questions in regard to that situation when you didn't let faith guide you.

Let's consider the consequences of not exercising our faith.

- What did you gain by worrying about your situation?
- What did fear keep you from doing?
- How stressed did you allow yourself to become?
- Did your daily obligations suffer because you just couldn't focus?
- What kinds of self-defeating thoughts were going through your mind?
- Were you able to be fully present with your family?
- Were you able to function at work?
- Did you lose sleep?

As you reflect on the times in which you did not exercise faith and surrendered to worry, doubt, and fear, you should acknowledge that letting those negative emotions consume you did nothing to improve your situation. As a matter of fact, those things typically make your situation worse. We often fail to act and are completely stressed in the process. Clearly, not having faith in those stressful situations neither benefits nor serves you in any way.

After reflecting on those past deficiencies of faith, you should be able to see how insufficient faith really restricts your ability to function. You likely will build a very strong conviction that you do not want to go through that again. There is nothing joyful about it, and it sucks the energy right out of you, draining you of your drive and willingness to keep pursuing your dreams. A lack of faith will not produce the results you want.

Let's take that lesson and apply it to something you may be facing right now. Is anything in your life wearing you down? There is no better time than the present to start practicing what faith can do for your life. You cannot force a problem to be solved if it has to run its course. But you can turn over your worries to your faith.

When you exercise faith, you don't worry about things that are not in your control. The majority of things we worry about never come to fruition anyway. Faith and fear cannot coexist. One gives way to the other. Either you move in faith or you are paralyzed by fear.

When you have faith, you act even though you don't have it all figured out, even if your circumstances are shouting that it's not possible. When you have faith, things work out in your favor, and you come out of your situation a much stronger person than you were going in. In faith, even failure is a step forward.

For some people, faith seems to come naturally. Perhaps they have been practitioners for many years. Others must learn faith in the hour of need and nurture it. That's okay. The greater the need, the deeper faith will take root, and the faster it will grow.

Some great ways to exercise your faith:

- *Strengthen your prayer life.* You've probably heard by now that prayer changes things. Yes, it does! Pray to God and let Him know you're struggling. Ask for guidance and strength. If this does not come naturally to you, don't worry. It doesn't have to be eloquent for God to hear you. Prayer is not a matter of getting God's attention—God knows all about you already. It's about preparing yourself to receive what He has planned for you.

- *Keep a prayer journal.* Write down the things you are requesting in prayer. When your prayers have been answered, go back and record exactly how the answer came. This will serve as evidence that God hears prayer. It will help you strengthen your prayer life, especially if you currently lack one.

- *Monitor your feelings of worry and fear.* Typically when those feelings begin to surface, your faith has wavered. Remember, fear and faith cannot exist together. One gives way to the other. When we experience fear, we have to intentionally take steps of faith, even though it may be difficult.

- *Surround yourself with people who have battle-tested faith.* Ask them questions and observe how they walk in faith during their trials. They will serve as a powerful example of what it means to truly have faith.

- *Reflect on a challenge you had in the past in which your faith saw you through.* Remind yourself of that experience and of how things worked in your favor. We have a tendency to forget about the times in which our faith prevailed, especially when we face a new life challenge. I've been guilty of this myself.

I would love to assure you that once you have faith, you will no longer experience trying moments in life, but that isn't the case. I can assure you that with faith, you can make it through the toughest times and endure whatever life throws at you.

Why allow yourself to be paralyzed by fear, doubt, and worry when you have the capacity to harness your faith and push through any circumstance? Faith makes it possible for you to show up for your life.

FAITH IN MOTION

" *If patience is worth anything, it must endure to the end of time. And a living faith will last in the midst of the blackest storm.*

Mahatma Gandhi

Have you ever heard a story that rattled you so badly you couldn't get it out of your mind? Not only was the story shocking, but the people involved in the story responded in a way that was so unusual, it was almost impossible to understand. The truth is, when tragedy hits us and our faith is tested to the extreme, nobody knows how we will react. Will we abandon our faith or will we cling to it, as if it were our last breath?

One day, I was driving in my car, listening to a radio talk show, and thinking about what I had going on for that day. A special guest, J. J. Jasper, came on the show along with his wife. The radio host, Chris Fabry, asked JJ to share his story, and I tuned in to the radio a bit closer, wondering what it may be. What he shared was spellbinding, beyond anything I was expecting at that moment.

JJ, a radio DJ and an impressive speaker, talked about how he had what many would consider an amazing life, with a wonderful marriage and five beautiful children. He lived on a spectacular horse and cattle farm. One sunny Friday, he and his only son, five-year-old Cooper, decided to go for a ride in their dune buggy, just as they'd done so many times before. He strapped Cooper in, did the same for himself, and they drove off.

They drove around most of the afternoon and had a great time. Eventually, it was time to get back to the house and end the day's off-road adventure.

Cooper said, "Flame on, Dad!" This was their code phrase for doing a few donuts in their dune buggy before heading in. Smiling and ready to enjoy their end-of-ride routine, JJ turned the wheel of the dune buggy and gave it some extra gas so it would spin around and kick up the dirt, something that made them both laugh. But that's not what happened on this day. Instead, the dune buggy tipped over and rolled—and although it had a protective metal cage, something went terribly wrong.

JJ got up, immediately looked over at his son and asked, "You okay, buddy?"

There was no answer. JJ quickly unstrapped Cooper from the harness and began to administer CPR, but it was too late. Little Cooper's neck had been broken in the accident. In that single moment of fun, something that was common for JJ and Cooper, his family changed forever.

It's so hard to imagine, and it still brings a lump to my throat, when I reflect on how I felt as I first heard JJ tell this story.

It was such a sad story, especially after hearing so much about how Cooper was an outgoing little boy. That picture of a vibrant

114

little personality made it instantly seem more personal to me. What was even more shocking is that JJ and his wife still have a strong marriage. Statistically speaking, most marriages do not survive this type of tragedy. JJ and his wife hadn't turned to drugs, and they were not bitter or angry at God.

I pulled over to the side of the road to listen to them finish the interview. I was entranced by every word, wondering how they had found the strength to go on.

JJ and his wife had decided to share their story as a way to help others find hope in the midst of tragedy. They have helped thousands. Don't get me wrong, it is very clear that JJ and his wife are in deep pain over the loss of their only son. But their faith is stronger than the pain. Although they went through one of the worst tragedies anyone could experience, they have the faith to endure. They use that faith to bring hope and healing into the lives of others.

JJ's story was an enormous demonstration of faith to me. It proved that, with the right amount of faith, we have the capacity to overcome whatever life throws our way.

Faith can help us overcome pain, worry, difficulty, and the worst circumstances. Faithful people hope and believe that somehow, some way, God will see them through any situation, no matter how difficult or unpromising it may appear. Faith is one of the most important tools for overcoming challenges. Without it, showing up for your life is almost impossible. You should pursue it with all that you have in you.

EIGHT

THE EXTRAORDINARY YOU

> " *The difference between ordinary and extraordinary is that little extra.*
>
> Jimmy Johnson

With a grateful heart and a profound appreciation for what I am blessed to do day in and day out, I am humbled and joyful that you are reading this book. It means you have chosen to show up for your life.

An entirely new outlook awaits you, one that will take you from living an ordinary life to an extraordinary life. Let it be known that you already have the ability inside of you to implement the principles shared in this book. I am simply hoping the ideas and stories I've shared have equipped you to start implementing those principles today. We have all been granted life, and it is a very amazing gift. But ultimately, what we choose to do with our gift is up to us. I hope that you choose to embrace yours and use it.

We will all face challenges and setbacks on occasion. Most times, we will not be able to control the circumstances—but we do get to determine how we will respond. We will decide whether we are going to rise to the occasion and persevere, or whether we are going to surrender our goals and dreams to the obstacles before us. All of our power lies in what we choose to do at that moment, and how we respond.

The way we show up during those moments in our lives is the fundamental difference between being the victim of our circumstances or the victor of our lives. I truly hope the seven principles I've laid out for you in this book have shown you what's required for you to show up for your life and to make the transition from an ordinary to an extraordinary life.

Let me remind you that choosing to show up doesn't mean your life is going to be any easier. In fact, life will still present you with obstacles, disappointments, and unforeseen setbacks. Applying the principles that you've started learning in this book will put you in the elite company of those who have resolved to show up for their lives in spite of the circumstances, despite failure and disappointment, despite fear and doubt, and regardless of unforeseen challenges presented by life.

Only a special kind of individual can take that type of stand—an individual like you, willing to invest in yourself by taking the time to read through this entire book with honest and sincere intentions. You are getting the big picture, and that will lead to even bigger things.

If, by chance, you have fallen short or failed to show up in any area of your life in the past, let me remind you that you now have the essential principles to turn it all around. In the past, your excuses never really served you, but you accepted them. Resorting to those excuses definitely will not serve you because you are fully equipped to make the best of your life, regardless of what you may have to overcome. This is your moment of truth, and you must decide if, from this moment forward, you are going to show up for your life.

Will you align yourself with what you have been called to do with your life? Will you identify some compelling reasons worth fighting for as you pursue your goals and dreams? Will you maintain the right mindset to handle the devastating hits in life? Will you learn to accept the process as you go through your personal journey of fulfillment? Will you abandon all of your excuses and be unstoppable in your pursuit? Will you build and learn to draw from your faith, especially during the moments when your circumstances present obstacles to your goals?

Will you show up for your life?

REVIEW

To send you off fully prepared to show up for your life, let's revisit the principles we learned in this book:

1. SHOWING UP

Frankly, nothing happens until you are at least willing to show up. If you haven't been showing up consistently or, even worse, you haven't been showing up at all, it's time for a change. It's time to stack the odds in your favor.

The fundamental points attached to showing up are:

a. *Decide.* Nothing happens until you decide. Decide this day that you are going to show up. No more excuses. No more standing on the sidelines. It's time to make the conscious decision to show up.

b. *Find a compelling reason.* One thing is certain: Once you decide to show up, you are going to encounter challenges and roadblocks. Therefore, you had better have a compelling reason to stick to the course and keep pushing forward. What reasons make it worth it for you to endure the trial and continue to fight?

c. *Take action.* You may not have all the steps figured out, but that doesn't exempt you from taking action. Identify at least one step you can take, no matter how small, that will move you in the direction of your goal.

2. DEFINE YOUR PURPOSE

It's hard to show up when your life has no clear purpose. You do yourself a large disservice when you drift through life subscribing to someone else's vision rather than seeking and formulating your own. This often leads to discontentment and internal frustration. Why not position yourself to win by actively seeking and pursuing your purpose? Finding your purpose is essential for living a fulfilling life, one that you have often only imagined in your dreams.

The fundamental points attached to determining our purpose are:

a. *Become more self-aware.* Think about what's brewing inside of you and discover your special God-given gifts and talents. Explore those and watch how a fundamental shift in your outlook regarding the future begins to formulate. Life is so much easier when you're driven by purpose.

b. *Take your blinders off.* Become more aware of the ways that you can not only find but also live your purpose. It's about more than just money, a big house, and security—it's about true fulfillment, which is not to be confused with achievement. There are many people who have achieved a great deal, but they are not fulfilled because they are not living their purpose.

c. *Do the work.* You have to be intentional about finding your purpose. You cannot sit on the sidelines and expect it to come. It requires you to search both within and without, and it may take some time to come to you.

d. *Claim your purpose.* Don't hesitate to put your stake in the ground and proclaim your purpose once you find it. Knowing your purpose and deciding not to claim it does you no good. If it's yours, don't be concerned with naysayers. Claim it and take action.

e. *Take responsibility.* We have each been put on this earth for a unique purpose. No other person in this world can live out your purpose for you because it is specific to you. No one else will start your business, write your book, or make the type of contribution that only you can make with your gifts and talents. It's ultimately your responsibility to both find and live out your purpose.

3. KNOW YOUR *WHY*

After we find our purpose, we need fuel to keep us going in our pursuit of it. Your *why* is a compelling reason you can draw from during those difficult moments when you become tired, frustrated, discouraged, or even contemplate giving up. A powerful *why* provides you with the mental and physical fuel you need to keep pushing forward.

Without a clearly defined *why*, obstacles and setbacks can seem insurmountable and lead us to abandon our goals and dreams prematurely. It's important that we make sure our *why* is deeply planted in our hearts. You must ensure it remains at the forefront of your mind to combat any self-defeating thoughts and to assist you in weathering the storms you may face.

The fundamental points attached to knowing your *why* are:

a. *Recognize what is driving your current actions.* When you are pursuing a goal or dream, take a moment to clearly identify why you are doing it. Many times, we find ourselves in the middle of the pursuit without knowing exactly why we are doing it. An unclear *why* will rarely get you to the finish line.

b. *Think about what's most important to you.* Is it a family member who is counting on you? Is it the desire to change your legacy? Is it the desire to make a contribution greater than yourself? Is it simply seeking greater fulfillment from life? Whatever it is, it's worth taking the time to identify it based on your personal values and beliefs.

c. *Give yourself a strong visual reminder of your why.* Then make it a part of you. A well-planted image or thought is a sound strategic step in making sure your *why* never slips away from your thoughts when you need it most.

d. *Remember WHY:* <u>W</u>atching is not an option. <u>H</u>oping alone is not enough. <u>Y</u>ou are the difference.

e. *Anchor to your why.* As you pursue your goals and dreams, use your *why* to drive you through any challenges or obstacles you may encounter.

4. ANTICIPATE THE HITS

Even if you are completely clear on your purpose, and you have established your *why*, life will still present you with some devastating hits. It can be a painful experience to receive an unexpected setback or loss. It's like getting the wind knocked out of you. It catches you completely off guard and often leaves you feeling overwhelmed and even defeated. Although we all wish we could avoid taking the hits in life, they are, unfortunately, often outside of our control.

Once we accept the fact that we can't just simply avoid them, we have one other choice—to prepare for them. We have to do our best to prepare mentally to deal with unanticipated hits. Even when attempting to cope, we may still feel overwhelmed when tragedy or disappointment happens. The key is to reduce our recovery time and not allow ourselves to be taken out of the game.

The fundamental points attached to anticipating the hits are:

a. *Have an adaptable plan of action.* When you get an unanticipated hit, you don't have to quit what you are striving to achieve. There is always something you can do to help you keep moving forward, because you are committed to showing up.

b. *Deal with adversity proactively and not reactively.* We gather knowledge, strength, and the grit to keep working toward what is most important to us by being proactively prepared.

c. *Gratitude.* Draw strength from everything you are grateful for when times are hard. Realize that you are not alone. Every person has challenges, yet some people have risen above the unanticipated hits and have gone on to do great things. You can be one of those people too!

d. *Courage.* Remember that you are human. You will make mistakes, but you will also have the chance to learn from them, just as you can learn from success. Basically, we can all learn from everything in life as long as we are showing up.

5. TRUST THE PROCESS

One of the biggest concerns many of us have when life delivers hits is whether we will be able to endure. Will things work out in the end? We often become frustrated, impatient, and miss opportunities for growth. This makes it essential to remember the fifth principle.

It is inevitable that we will have to go through seasons in our lives that will place us outside of our comfort zone and require us to stretch and grow. Those seasons can become even more challenging when we question everything along the way, failing to trust that things will work out in our favor.

We must learn to trust the process, knowing that somehow, some way, God is going to work things out. When all is said and done, we will recognize that what He did was in our favor. This can be challenging because we are often seeking a shortcut or attempting to skip the process altogether. But it's all necessary for our growth.

The fundamental points attached to trusting the process are:

a. *Have faith.* Physical evidence of faith seldom exists in the midst of struggles. We must be driven by a belief in our hearts and minds that everything will work out.

b. *Don't let other people's words seal your fate.* When someone thinks you should give up your dreams, they may not be intentionally trying to sabotage you. They simply do not know what's inside of you. They have no idea what can happen if you continue to have faith while doing everything in your power to make it through any situation you are facing.

c.   *Life doesn't resolve its problems on your timetable.* Some processes that need to take place are out of your control.

d.   *Build patience.* You may not have any patience or even like the thought of having patience, but it is necessary. Patience can be learned. It is like a muscle: The more you use it, the stronger it gets.

e.   *Live by the mantra of acceptance, attitude, and action.* These are the three A's that will enable you to trust the process and deepen your faith. When you accept the things you cannot change, maintain a positive attitude, and continue to take action, things always work out during the process.

6. BE UNSTOPPABLE

When we miss the mark or fall short of our goals and dreams, it often comes down to one simple thing—we stopped. Sure, we may have found some great excuses to justify why we decided to stop, but it still doesn't change the fact that we quit. Gave up.

If you intend to show up for your life and accomplish your goals and dreams, you must implement the sixth principle. When you are unstoppable, you no longer make excuses. Quitting is no longer an option and, no matter what challenges come into your life, you find a way to get around them or break through them.

Being unstoppable means that you are committed to taking relentless action in the direction of your goals and dreams, and you find a way to overcome every obstacle. It's the mindset that, when fully embodied, takes you through the finish line.

The fundamental points attached to being unstoppable are:

a.   *Stop making excuses.* Do not justify why you failed to reach your goal. No excuses are valid. You can either makes excuses or produce results. You cannot do both.

b.   *Prepare to be uncomfortable, unrealistic, and unstoppable.* If you don't, it'll be your undoing, and you'll be the spectator instead of the participant in your own life.

Doing great things is not always comfortable, and your dreams won't always seem realistic. You need to mentally declare that you will be unstoppable.

c. *Show the world what you've got.* Be prepared to be called crazy and a dreamer. It comes with the territory. If people around you are not questioning your goals and dreams, then maybe you are not dreaming big enough.

d. *If you want something bad enough, you will fight for it.* It becomes a part of you, and you can't even imagine yourself being disconnected from it. Some may look at and call your strong desire "being crazy." We call it being unstoppable.

e. *Create milestones.* As you pursue your goals and dreams, short- and long-term milestones give you a valuable sense of progress. Being unstoppable means making continuous progress throughout your journey.

f. *Stay committed.* Remember George Zalucki's words, "Commitment is doing the thing you said you would do, long after the mood you said it in has left you." Your emotions will vary and waver throughout the process. Nevertheless, honor your commitment to being unstoppable.

7. HAVE FAITH

Even after making the commitment to be unstoppable, it can feel as if things are just not working in your favor. This is particularly true when your circumstances don't seem promising or when your progress doesn't seem very impressive. There are times when it will seem you have no physical evidence that things are going to work. In those moments, faith is your strongest weapon.

In times of worry, fear, and doubt, your faith will see you through. "Faith is the evidence of things not seen." Faith is holding on to your dreams, working relentlessly toward them, even when you cannot see progress. Even when no one encourages you or validates your vision. Even when rejection follows rejection. No matter what, God has the ability to work in your favor. In those critical moments, faith will see you through. Your faith is essential if you want to show up for your life.

The fundamentals of faith:

a. *Faith is one of the single most important elements in your life.* Faith enables you to keep pushing forward even in the seemingly worst times. It fortifies you and gives you hope, especially in situations that appear to be hopeless.

b. *Everything works out in its own time.* When we waste time craving things to work out right now, it casts our focus in a negative direction. We have no control over the timing of our success. Don't let yourself be discouraged. Keep pushing toward your goal.

c. *The best example you give others arises from your faith.* Think of the most inspiring stories you've ever heard, including the ones in this book. You can see how faith made the difference between success and failure.

d. *In trials, faith is solidified.* When you hold fast to your faith that all will turn in your favor, despite any evidence to the contrary, that's when the true value of faith is revealed.

e. *Keep in mind the times when you relied on faith in the past.* Reflect on a situation in the past when you had to depend on your faith, and things worked out. Remember that experience and how you initially felt compared with how you felt afterward, when things eventually worked out for you. When facing a new challenge, we tend to forget about the times in the past when our faith allowed us to persevere.

f. *The antidote to fear is faith.* Remember faith conquers fear because the two cannot coexist. The next time you're feeling fearful, remember to tap into your faith.

Our faith is essential in helping us to navigate difficult times. It somehow manages to preserve us and gives us hope in the most unpromising circumstances. All of us will have to draw from our faith at some point in our lives.

Sadly, most people will go through life in quiet desperation, as Henry David Thoreau said, wishing they had reached their full potential, wishing they had taken a stand, wishing they had shown up. You are no longer in the category of most people. You have taken the time to read this book, and now you are equipped to show up for your life.

It's time to

... Leave mediocrity behind

... Be the victor in your life rather than the victim

... Overcome your circumstances and challenges

... Live a life of purpose and fulfillment

... Go from ordinary to extraordinary

It's time to show up for your life.

Show up!

ACKNOWLEDGMENTS

This book is the result of tremendous love and support. I want to acknowledge my beautiful wife, Casandra, for her unwavering love and support and for being my number one cheerleader. I want to acknowledge my mom for her immeasurable love and for inspiring the core message of this book. I want to acknowledge Les Brown for writing the foreword to this book and for paving the way for my speaking and coaching business.

I want to acknowledge Star Bobatoon and Louis Moorer for their commitment to the Show Up For Your Life Movement and years of support and encouragement. I want to acknowledge Tiger Sun for his creative genius and for being such an intricate part of my business team. And finally, I want to acknowledge the Show Up For Your Life Movement members for their ongoing support and for reminding me on a daily basis of the significance of my work. Thank you, all.

ABOUT THE AUTHOR

Andy Henriquez is a strategic storytelling expert, speaker, and coach who has the unique gift of crafting and delivering transformational messages that leave a lasting impact on his audience. His spellbinding delivery style and power-packed content is the reason world-renowned motivational speaker Les Brown affectionately refers to him as "The Great One."

Whether standing on stage and captivating an audience with his heartfelt and compelling message or conducting workshops and training, Andy's impact resonates with audiences worldwide. His experience and accomplishments are diverse and vast, giving him a special ability to relate to all audiences.

Andy was born to Haitian immigrants who moved to the United States in pursuit of the American Dream. With the core values of hard work, discipline, and commitment instilled by his parents, he attended Florida State University, graduating summa cum laude in Accounting. As a licensed CPA, Andy worked for the prestigious accounting firm, PricewaterhouseCoopers LLP. A risk taker and businessman at heart, Andy left the firm in 2004 to fulfill his destiny as an entrepreneur, speaker, and coach.

Andy is known for delivering messages that go beyond the mind and penetrate the heart of audiences. A sought-after speaker and trainer, he has spoken to thousands of people ranging from corporate, nonprofit, direct sales, and personal development seminar audiences.

To learn more about Andy, his products or coaching, visit www.AndyHenriquez.com.

IT'S TIME TO CASH IN ON YOUR STORY

ANDY HENRIQUEZ | STRATEGIC STORYTELLING EXPERT

Great entrepreneurs, leaders, coaches, CEOs, authors, salespeople, and speakers all have one thing in common. **They are great storytellers.**

They understand that in order to influence people and move them to action, you have to be able to share compelling stories.

The effective use of stories can help you to increase your sales, gain more influence, close more deals, attract more donors, enroll more people into your vision, gain a competitive advantage and ultimately produce better results.

Andy Henriquez is a strategic storytelling expert. Whether standing on stage and captivating an audience with heartfelt and compelling stories or conducting workshops and trainings on effective storytelling, no one harnesses the power of story like Andy.

Andy gives your organization the customized experience it deserves and provides practical strategies for leveraging the power of story. Inspire your organization and equip them to increase sales, improve fundraising, connect with customers and stand out in the market place with a heartfelt keynote or strategic storytelling workshop with Andy.

"Andy Henriquez has a unique gift of going beyond the mind of the audience and penetrating their hearts which is something that very few speakers have the ability to do. That is why I often refer to him as, "The Great One." If you are looking for a lasting impact on your organization along with practical methods, techniques and strategies to take your team to the next level, Andy is your man."

Les Brown
World-renowned Motivational Speaker

"Andy, you are a genius and a master at what you do. My VIP Day training with you has dramatically changed my presentation skills and my overall confidence. You helped me identify the universal themes in my stories and to deliver them in such a way to create impact and produce results. The time I spent learning from you is some of the most rewarding and beneficial hours of my life. My only regret is that I didn't work with you sooner. Thank you."

Marlene Gordon
Vice President, General Counsel, Bacardi North America Corporation

Here are just a few organizations that have retained Andy's services

Bring Andy In for:

Keynote Presentations   Consulting
Coaching   Breakout Sessions
Workshops/Seminars   Staff Trainings

Schedule a Discovery Call With Andy Now:
www.DiscoveryCallWithAndy.com

Show Up For Your Life LLC - www.AndyHenriquez.com - Andy@AndyHenriquez.com